The
SCARIFICATION

The Facial Scarification in South Sudan

Discipleship Press

Website: www.discipleshippress.wordpress.com
Email: maluthabiel@gmail.com
Phone: +254 110 424 822
~~***~~
P.O. Box 28448-00100, Nairobi, Kenya
ISBN-13: 978-1475065640

Library of Congress Control Number: 2022907957

DEDICATION

This book is dedicated to my father, Maluth Abiel Kueth.

His care shaped me, and his counsel steadied me, even when I did not listen.

He advised me not to receive scarification marks on my forehead, but I still chose them under peer pressure.

So I write this book as a tribute to him, and as a small repayment for a debt I can never fully repay.

Thank you, Father, for your love, your sacrifices, and the way you kept guiding me even when I resisted.

ACKNOWLEDGEMENTS

I thank the people who helped this book come into being, through mentorship, memory, correction, and steady encouragement.

I am grateful to Francis Ayul Nyok for mentorship and influence.

I acknowledge my uncles and elders, including Chol Deng Awuor, Achuil Nyok Lual, and Deng Akech Deng, for direct contributions.

I also thank Mut Peter Nyak, Elijah Kueth Malou, Gatluak Deng Reath, Eliza Ayak Ruei, and Puok Deng for support during the writing.

I appreciate Paul Puur Miyen, Chany Nyok Dhic, Peter Bol Lem, Elijah Akol Minyang, and Upendo, a sister-friend from Tanzania who nicknamed me Gäärman.

And I acknowledge Maluth Abiel for contributions that mattered more than he may realize.

AUTHOR'S NOTE

This is a personal story before it is anything else.

Yes, I spoke with people and listened to elders, but I am not presenting this as a fully researched account.

I am telling the story of the marks on my forehead, received when I was fifteen, and how that single moment became a turning point in my life.

This book sits in my Autobiography Series because it is one of the main events that shaped my identity, my choices, and how I see culture, pressure, and consequence.

If you read it as a cultural account, you will still find meaning. But I hope you read it first as a human account, because that is how it happened to me.

SIMPLE TIMELINE
Age fifteen: I received the scarification marks on my forehead.

Afterward: I carried the marks into my later years, and the memory of my father's counsel kept returning until it pushed me to write this book.

CONTENTS

PART I
CHAPTER 1: THE BOY WHO WANTED A GOOD NAME

I have learned that some decisions do not begin on the day you make them. They begin quietly, like a small fire hidden under ash. For a long time, you do not call it a decision. You call it a wish. You call it a dream. You call it a plan for the future. Yet, one day, the hidden fire rises and becomes a flame, and that flame demands a direction. That is how it was for me with scarification.

When I look back, I can trace the first thread to one simple hunger. I wanted a respected and honorable standing among our people. I wanted a good name. I did not have those words in my mouth every morning, but they lived in my chest. They lived in the way I listened when older men spoke. They lived in the way I watched how people greeted certain families, and how a name could open doors in a village without any money changing hands. They lived in the way boys like me studied the social air of our community, trying to learn what makes a man valued.

A good name, where I come from, is not only your personal character. It is also how you are seen among your people. It is reputation. It is a form of belonging. It is a kind of safety. It is the difference between being a boy who is always questioned and a young man whose words are given space. It is the difference between being laughed at in public and being listened to. It is the difference between being treated as someone's child and being treated as someone who can carry responsibility.

In my younger mind, I believed there were visible signs that could speed that journey. I believed there were acts that could announce you before you even spoke. I believed there were marks that could say, "This one belongs to the men." And because I believed that, my hunger for a good name naturally turned toward the practices that our community linked to manhood.

One of those practices was scarification. It was not just something people did. It was a symbol. It was a public line between boyhood and manhood, between childhood fear and the courage we claimed. It

1

carried a social meaning that was bigger than the physical cuts. It was one of those things you could not hide if it was done on the forehead. You carried it into every greeting, every gathering, every argument, every celebration. It sat on your face like a statement.

As boys, we were not raised in silence about bravery. Bravery was spoken of openly. It was praised. It was expected. In our world, fearlessness was something we aspired to wear, not only for ourselves, but for the pride of the community that raised us. We learned early that courage is not merely private. It is a public currency. People speak of it. People measure it. People teach it as if it can be poured from elders into the hearts of boys.

So we listened to stories. We listened to accounts of men who stood firm in moments of danger. We listened to stories of endurance. Those stories were not only history. They were education. They were training for the soul. They were a kind of social schooling that shaped what a boy considered admirable. And when you hear those stories while you are still trying to become someone, the stories do not stay as stories. They become mirrors. You start asking where you fit.

I do not want to pretend I was different from other boys. I was a boy growing up among boys, and boys compete even when nobody says the word "competition." They compare themselves, even when they are laughing. They test each other, even when they are playing. They form rankings in their minds. Who is bold? Who is timid? Who can endure discomfort? Who cries quickly? Who can take a joke without anger? Who can take pain without showing weakness? Those questions live in boyhood like invisible judges.

When scarification came into our conversations, it came with those judges.

It came as a measure. It came as an examination. It came as something that could seal your status in the eyes of your peers. It came as something that could protect you from mockery. It came as something that could earn you respect. And if you are a boy with a hunger for a good name, you are easily pulled toward whatever your world offers as a shortcut to honor.

That is the part many people understand easily. They hear "scarification," and they think, "Of course, it is about culture." But for me, the deeper truth was not only culture. The deeper truth was the need to belong. It was the fear of being the odd one. It was the anxiety of being left behind by my age-mates. It was the desire to be seen as strong, not only in front of elders, but also among the boys whose opinions seemed to matter more than they should have.

Peer pressure played a major role in my decision, even though my father opposed it. That one line carries a lot of weight, because it is one of the hardest truths to admit. Many of us prefer to believe our choices come only from our inner convictions. We like to say, "I chose." But sometimes the choice is made inside a crowd. Sometimes you choose, but the crowd is standing inside your mind when you choose. Sometimes you are not trying to impress yourself. You are trying to impress the faces around you.

My father refused to consent, yet I remained fixed in my decision, driven by the need to fit in with my age-mates.

When I write that now, I feel both respect and regret at the same time. Respect, because my father saw something I did not see. Regret, because I was too young to understand the kind of love that refuses, even when it could have been easier to simply allow the boy to follow the crowd.

At fifteen, you can mistake refusal for hostility. You can think your father is blocking your destiny. You can think he is embarrassed by you. You can think he is out of touch with the times. You can think he does not understand the social world you are living in every day. You can interpret his "no" as a personal attack. You can turn his caution into your rebellion.

That is what stubbornness does. It turns guidance into a wall. And when you are stubborn, you do not only resist. You also demand "evidence." You want long explanations. You want arguments. You want a debate that you can win. You want your father to speak in a way that matches the noise inside your head.

I wanted "evidence." I wanted arguments strong enough to break my own hunger for belonging.

But a father does not always argue. Sometimes he simply refuses. Sometimes he has already seen enough of life to know that a child does not need a speech. A child needs protection. A child needs a boundary. A child needs someone older to take the blame for being unpopular.

Looking back, I realize that my father's refusal was not the absence of love. It was love without decoration. It was love that did not beg to be accepted. It was love that was willing to be misunderstood, if misunderstanding could keep me safe from a choice I might later regret.

Still, I was fifteen. And fifteen has its own logic. The logic of fifteen is simple: what your peers admire becomes what you admire. What your peers mock becomes what you fear. What your peers reward becomes what you chase. The approval of your age-mates becomes a kind of daily bread. You eat it or you starve inside. That is how it feels, even if it is not the full truth.

When my age-mates were moving toward scarification, the pressure was not only spoken pressure. It was also silent pressure. Silence can pressure you more than words. When everybody is doing something, and you are the one not doing it, you start feeling like your body is a question mark. You start feeling like your face will be a joke. You start feeling like your presence will invite commentary. And a boy who wants a good name fears that kind of commentary more than he fears the blade itself.

So, in my mind, the decision was dressed as courage. I told myself I was choosing bravery. I told myself I was choosing manhood. I told myself I was choosing dignity. I told myself I was choosing identity.

And yes, there is a part of it that is courage. There is pain involved. There is endurance involved. There is self-control involved. There is the ability to stay still, to resist screaming, to resist running, to resist shame. In that sense, it can be called a test.

But I also know now that courage is not always a clean thing. Sometimes courage is mixed with fear. Sometimes courage is mixed with pride. Sometimes courage is mixed with the need to be accepted. Sometimes courage is not the pure desire to do what is right. Sometimes it is the desire to avoid being called weak.

This is why I say the decision did not begin on the day it happened. It began in the hunger for a good name. It began in the social air that taught boys what should be admired. It began in the stories that made pain look like a badge. It began in the fear of being left behind. And it began in my refusal to accept my father's refusal.

When you are fifteen, you rarely imagine the "after." You think about the ceremony, the applause, the respect, the new identity. You do not think about the long years of carrying the marks into places where people do not share your culture. You do not think about how a symbol can become a label. You do not think about how your face can speak before you speak.

At that time, all I could see was the social door I believed scarification would open. I wanted that door open because I wanted the feeling of being fully included among my peers.

And that hunger can be strong enough to make you ignore even the people you love most.

I sometimes ask myself what exactly I thought would happen if I refused scarification. Would the world end? Would I be excluded forever? Would I be unable to marry? Would I be unable to lead? Would I be treated as a child even when I became an adult? The mind of a boy can exaggerate social consequences. It can treat mockery like a death sentence. It can treat jokes like a permanent curse.

In that boyhood thinking, scarification became the solution to a problem that was partly real and partly imagined. Real, because societies do reward conformity, and people do value shared identity. Imagined, because a human being's worth is bigger than peer approval, and manhood is bigger than a ritual. But a boy does not always see that. A boy sees the next gathering. A boy sees the next joke. A boy sees the next comment. And a boy can sacrifice his future self to protect his present pride.

That is why this chapter is not only about scarification. It is about the hunger for a good name. It is about the boy who believed a symbol could give him status. It is about the boy who did not know how to stand alone. It is about the boy who did not know how to say, "I will be respected in a different way." It is about the boy who did not yet understand that real respect does not always come from what you do to your body, but from what you do with your life.

And yet, I do not want to write this as if I am only condemning my younger self. That would be dishonest. There was meaning in it too, even if that meaning came with cost. Scarification, in the minds of many in our communities, stands for identity. It stands for belonging. It stands for continuity. It is tied to history. It is tied to how people understand themselves as a people.

So my younger self was not chasing something meaningless. He was chasing belonging. He was chasing a form of identity. He was chasing what he believed was honor. He just did not understand the full shape of what he was chasing.

There is another confession I want to make early, because it reveals how deeply peer approval had shaped my thinking. Later, after the marks were already part of my face, I discovered that I even felt disappointment about the size of my scars. I wanted the scars to be bigger. I wanted them to look louder. I wanted them to say more.

That is a painful thing to admit, because it shows that the ritual was not only about identity. It was also about display. It was also about being noticed. It was also about competition, even in pain.

And I am not proud of that part.

But I include it because it is true, and because it reveals the kind of boy I was. I was not only trying to be a man. I was also trying to be seen. And when a boy's goal is to be seen, he can become dissatisfied even with what is already permanent on his face. He can start wishing for more, as if more pain would produce more respect.

Time corrected that foolishness.

Time taught me that the worth of the scars was not in their size, but in what they carried. They carried a story about courage, yes. They also carried a story about pressure, choice, and the long road between boyhood and wisdom.

I learned that the face can carry a lesson for the heart.

I learned that sometimes the mark you chase becomes the teacher you did not expect.

I learned that identity is not something you receive once and for all. Identity continues to grow, even after the blade, even after the ceremony, even after the applause fades. Identity grows when you learn how to interpret your own life honestly. Identity grows when you learn how to admit your weaknesses. Identity grows when you learn to honor your father's wisdom, even when you disobeyed it.

This is why my father's refusal returns again and again in my memory. At fifteen, I wanted him to fight me with words. I wanted him to argue with me. I wanted him to explain in a way that could satisfy my stubborn hunger for "evidence."

Now, I see the quiet strength in his refusal.

I see that he did not need to win a debate with a fifteen-year-old. He needed to plant a seed. That seed would grow later, after the ceremony, after the pride, after the disappointment, after the years.

If you are reading this and you are a young person, I want you to hear this carefully: it is possible to make a choice that wins the applause of your peers and still loses something inside you. It is possible to be praised and still be confused. It is possible to be called brave and still be driven mainly by fear. It is possible to pass a public test and still fail a private one.

That private test is the test of independence.

The test of being able to say no.

The test of being able to stand on your own feet even when your age-mates are walking in another direction.

I did not pass that private test at fifteen.

Instead, I chose to be included in the way my peers demanded.

This chapter, then, is about the beginning of that road. It is about the boy who wanted a good name. It is about the boy who confused public symbols with personal worth. It is about the boy who thought belonging must come through a blade. It is about the boy who did not understand that a father's refusal can be a gift.

Before the blade touched my forehead, the blade had already touched my thinking.

It had already shaped my idea of courage.

It had already shaped my idea of honor.

It had already shaped my idea of what it means to be a man.

And the hardest thing to admit is that the blade did not force itself on me. I walked toward it, believing I was walking toward a good name.

Yet, even now, after all these years, I am still learning what a good name truly is.

A good name is not just being marked.

A good name is not just being praised.

A good name is not just being included.

A good name is the kind of life that can look back at its choices without hiding.

A good name is the kind of man who can say, "I was pressured," and still not excuse himself.

A good name is the kind of person who can honor his father, not by pretending he always listened, but by admitting he did not, and by carrying the lesson forward.

That is where this story begins.

Not with the cuts.

Not with the ceremony.

Not with the blood.

But with a boy's hunger for a good name, and the quiet voice of a father who said no.

CHAPTER 2: MY FATHER SAID NO

When I say my father said no, I do not mean he said it with anger and shouting. I mean he said it with the calm authority of a man who had already walked through enough seasons to know that some choices look brave on the outside, yet they carry a weight that a boy cannot measure. His name is Maluth Abiel Kueth, and I have come to describe him as the kind of father whose care and counsel shape a child, even when that child refuses to listen.

At fifteen, I did not know how to respect a refusal I did not like. I thought respect meant agreement. I thought honor meant doing what elders did, not listening to a father who seemed to stand against what boys my age were calling manhood. I was too young to understand that a father's refusal is sometimes a gift that does not arrive wrapped in sweetness.

The truth, which I have stated plainly elsewhere in this book's early pages, is that my father advised me against receiving scarification marks on my forehead, and I still went ahead because peer pressure pulled harder than his counsel. That sentence is short, but it carries years inside it. It carries the story of a boy who wanted a good name, and a father who cared enough to risk being misunderstood by his own son.

The day I first heard his refusal, I did not feel gratitude. I felt blocked. I felt as if he was taking something from me. In my mind, scarification was not just a practice. It was a sign. It was a passport. It was a stamp on the forehead that could announce my inclusion before I even spoke. I saw it as a social protection. I saw it as a proof that I could endure pain without breaking. I saw it as a way to remove one more reason for other boys to look at me and feel superior.

My father did not see it the way I saw it. Or maybe he did see the social meaning, but he also saw the other side of it, the side I did not want to think about. Because when a boy is hungry for approval, he avoids thoughts that disturb his hunger. He tells himself only the parts that strengthen his plan. He pushes away warnings because warnings feel like insults to his courage.

My father did not sit me down and explain everything. In fact, one of my frustrations was that he never explained his reasoning in a way that could satisfy my stubborn mind. I wanted him to give me a list. I wanted him to fight my desire with arguments. I wanted him to produce what I called evidence, something concrete I could hold and show to my age-mates, something I could use as a shield when they laughed at my hesitation.

But fathers do not always argue with boys the way boys argue with boys. A father's "no" is often the end of his sentence. He is not trying to win a debate. He is trying to save a child. And sometimes, he saves that child by being firm, not by being persuasive.

At fifteen, that firmness felt like silence. And silence felt like disrespect. It felt like he did not take my desire seriously. It felt like he did not understand how much pressure I was under. Yet the older I became, the more I realized that his refusal was not careless silence. It was a controlled decision. It was a boundary. It was him drawing a line and saying, I will not encourage you into something you cannot undo.

There is a reason this chapter is placed early in the book. Scarification is the visible subject, but my father is one of the hidden subjects. This is also why I dedicated the book to him, because even now I see how his care has had an immeasurable impact on the person I became. Even my disobedience did not cancel his influence. In a strange way, it increased it, because his refusal became a voice in my mind that returned again and again whenever the marks on my forehead forced me to remember how I received them.

When a boy is about to step into a rite that many others have done, he thinks he is entering history. He thinks he is joining the line of men. He thinks he is completing what is expected. But a father, especially a father who has watched life closely, might also see the same rite as a doorway into avoidable suffering. He might see blood. He might see infection. He might see the future, where the boy will travel to places where those marks become a loud label. He might see the boy's face being read wrongly by people who do not know the language of his culture.

Even within our communities, scarification carries risks, and one of the most obvious risks is bleeding. I have written about my own experience with severe blood loss after receiving the marks. I remember how the bleeding was so heavy that, to onlookers, I appeared lifeless and could not respond to their questions. That is not a rumor I heard. That is my body. That is my memory. That is my life.

When I think about my father's refusal, I cannot separate it from that reality. It is possible that he knew stories of boys who bled excessively. It is possible he had heard the old fears that scarification could kill because of blood loss, fears that have been whispered through generations. Whether he believed those fears fully or not, he did not need to believe them fully to take them seriously. A father does not gamble with his child's life. Even a small chance of tragedy can be enough for him to say no.

And scarification, especially on the forehead, is not like a cut on the arm that can be hidden. It is a public cut. It is a cut that sits near the skull, and people have long believed that the skill of the elder practitioner matters deeply because guiding the blade wrongly could lead to catastrophic bleeding. People say many things in our societies. Some are exaggerated. Some are shaped by fear. Some are shaped by experience. But even when stories are not fully accurate, they often carry a warning. They carry the voice of earlier pain.

At fifteen, I did not care enough about warnings. I cared about acceptance.

So I pushed against my father's boundary. Not loudly, not with rebellion speeches, but with stubbornness that refused to move. I remained fixed in my decision, even though he refused to consent. That is one of the hardest admissions a son can write, because it makes you look small. It makes you look weak, not in courage, but in independence.

The strange thing about peer pressure is that it can make you feel strong while you are actually being controlled. It can make you feel like a leader while you are simply following. It can make you feel like a man while you are still a boy searching for approval.

In those days, I wanted to believe I was choosing scarification because I valued our culture. And I did value it, in my own youthful way. But if I am honest, the force that moved my feet toward the ceremony was not deep cultural study. It was not careful reflection. It was not a personal conviction that I could defend without the crowd behind me. It was the simple desire to fit in with my peers.

My father's refusal stood in the way of that desire, so I treated the refusal as an obstacle, not as love.

This is why I say I wanted "concrete evidence and rational arguments" from him. I did not want wisdom. I wanted tools for a debate. I wanted something I could carry into the circle of my age-mates. If he had given me that, I might have been able to delay, to pause, to retreat without losing face. At least that is what I told myself. But now, I am not sure. Sometimes, even when you are given evidence, you still choose the crowd. Because the problem is not lack of information. The problem is hunger.

Still, my father did not argue, and that made me feel free to continue. I interpreted his silence as weakness, as if he had no answer. But what if his silence was strength? What if he knew that the more he argued, the more I would resist, because resistance was already part of my pride?

Sometimes a father refuses and waits. He waits for time to teach what words cannot teach. He waits for experience to do its work. He waits for the child to grow into understanding.

That waiting can look like indifference when you are young, but it is not.

It is patience.

It is a painful patience because it means he must watch you choose what he fears, and he must still love you through it.

There is something else that makes my father's refusal even heavier to me now. In my early writing about this, I noted that several companions who joined me in receiving the marks on that occasion are no longer alive today, not because of scarification, but because of the wider turmoils that swallowed our war-torn homeland. Community conflicts, vengeance, animosity, the violence that makes boys into men too early, all of that claimed lives.

When I remember those companions, I think about how we stood together on that day, trying to prove something to the world. We did not know how quickly the world could turn against us. We did not know how many storms were waiting in front of our generation. We thought we were controlling one moment of pain, yet life was preparing years of pain that had nothing to do with a blade.

If my father had been able to speak to me from the future, he might have said, "My son, the land already has enough suffering. Do not add another suffering to your body, especially when it is not necessary." But he did not have to speak from the future. He was already a man, already experienced, already aware that life is unpredictable, already aware that war and social pressure can push boys into decisions they do not fully understand.

This is another reason I want to honor him. His refusal was not only about scarification. It was also about protecting me from unnecessary exposure to risk, in a land where risks are already everywhere.

When I speak of risk, I do not speak only of bleeding. I also speak of the social consequences that follow you. Later in my reflections, I observed acquaintances who seemed to age quickly because of heavy consumption of "aregi," the drink many know too well. I wrote that their deteriorating appearances made me appreciate that my own youthfulness has been preserved, and I connected that preservation to God's guidance rather than my own intelligence.

Why bring that here, in a chapter about my father?

Because it shows a pattern. Many young men think adulthood is proven by what you can endure, what you can consume, what you can survive. Some prove themselves through scarification. Some prove themselves through drink. Some prove themselves through fighting. The methods differ, but the hunger beneath is often the same: the hunger to be counted as a man.

A father who sees that hunger in his son might also see where it can lead. He might see the boy's desire for manhood turning into a lifetime of unnecessary tests. He might see the boy's weakness for peer approval becoming a trap that repeats itself in different forms.

So, when he says no to scarification, he is not only saying no to a ceremony. He is saying no to a mindset that believes manhood must be purchased through pain or performance.

I did not understand that at fifteen.

At fifteen, I was sure I knew what I wanted. And when you are sure, you become blind. You become deaf. You become skilled at ignoring anything that does not support your plan.

I look back now and I think of my father watching me. I imagine the quiet sadness he might have carried, the sadness of seeing his son moving toward a blade, not because he had to, but because other boys were moving toward it. I imagine him asking himself if his refusal would break our relationship. I imagine him choosing the refusal anyway because love is not always soft.

That kind of love is expensive. It costs the father peace.

It also costs the son time, because the son will only understand later.

After I received the marks and lived with them, my understanding began to change. It did not change in one day. It changed through small moments. It changed each time I noticed how permanent the marks were. It changed each time I remembered that my father had tried to protect me. It changed each time I saw how peer pressure can lead people into decisions they later regret.

In one of the passages that shaped my thinking later, I reflected on how societal pressure can become almost overwhelming, even for adolescent girls in other contexts, with some tying marriage commitments to completing prescribed rituals, only to face regret later when life changes. The point is not to compare sufferings. The point is to show that pressure can trap anyone, male or female, young or old, if the community makes acceptance feel conditional.

I wrote that embracing our diversity is important, but avoiding excessive pressure to force people into rigid conventions is equally important. That sentence is not theory to me. It is personal. It is my own forehead. It is my own decision at fifteen. It is my own father's refusal, standing there like a quiet wall I tried to break through.

If you are a parent reading this, you might wonder what you should do when your child is determined, when the crowd is loud, when culture is strong, when the child believes refusal is hate. I cannot write a perfect rule because life is not that clean. But I can say this: a father's guidance can still matter even when it is rejected.

I am proof of that.

My father refused to consent, and I still did it. That looks like failure on the surface. It looks like a father who could not control his son. But control is not the only measure of good parenting. Sometimes, the refusal is planted as a seed that will grow after the child has tasted the consequences.

My father's refusal became one of those seeds.

It grew into this book.

That is not a small thing. It means his "no" did not die on the day I disobeyed him. It kept living. It kept working in my memory. It kept returning each time I saw the marks, each time I felt the heat of regret, each time I remembered how quickly boys can become foolish when they are hungry for approval.

This is why, in my dedication, I wrote that I have been compelled to draft this book as a tribute to him, hoping to repay some debt of gratitude for his unwavering love and support. Even now, I feel that debt. A father gives you more than food. He gives you boundaries. He gives you protection you do not always recognize. He gives you a voice that follows you even when he is not near you.

It is possible that my father did not know all the technical details about scarification, about how elders guide the blade, about how oral knowledge is passed down from one generation to another. Or he may have known enough. I do not know exactly what he knew. What I do know is that he knew the most important thing: once the marks are on your forehead, they are not coming off.

A father also knows that regret does not remove marks.

A father knows that pain does not always prove wisdom.

A father knows that the crowd can be wrong.

And a father knows that a boy can be brave in the wrong direction.

So he said no.

At fifteen, I did not respect that no. I saw it as an obstacle, and I leaned harder into my desire to belong. I did not listen. I did not slow down. I did not pause long enough to ask myself why the one man whose love was closest to me was standing against my plan.

Now, I ask myself that question.

Why did he refuse?

Even if he never explained his reasons, the answer has become clearer with age. He refused because he loved me. He refused because he did not want me harmed. He refused because he could see risks I could not see. He refused because he knew boys can be driven by pressure more than by wisdom.

And because he refused, even though I disobeyed, I learned one of the hardest lessons of my life: a father's love can be right even when you do not understand it.

This chapter is not written to make my younger self look good. It is written to tell the truth. The truth is that my father gave me wise counsel and guidance, and I chose another voice, the voice of peers. The truth is that he did not consent, and I still went ahead. The truth is that I demanded evidence and arguments, when what I really needed was humility.

If you are a young reader, I want you to notice something here: sometimes your father's refusal is not a rejection of you. It is a protection of you. Sometimes your father sees the future better than you do, not because he is a prophet, but because he has already seen how life punishes unnecessary pride.

And if you are a father, I want you to know something too: even when your child rejects your counsel, your counsel can still live. It can still become a voice that returns later. It can still become a seed that grows.

My father's refusal lives in this book. It lives in the fact that I am able to look at my own forehead and speak honestly about why those marks are there. It lives in the fact that I can call peer pressure by its name without hiding. It lives in the fact that, even though I did not listen at fifteen, I am listening now, years later, with a heavier heart and a clearer mind.

In the next chapter, I will walk closer to the social world that pushed me, the voices of boys, the fear of being left out, the strange way a crowd can make a person forget his own mind. But before I move there, I want to leave this chapter with a simple confession.

Father, you were right to refuse.

And even though I did not listen then, I carry your counsel now, not only as regret, but as a guide.

Your "no" became part of my story, and part of my becoming.

CHAPTER 3: THE WEIGHT OF BELONGING

There are decisions that do not feel like decisions when you are a boy. They feel like gravity. They feel like the earth itself pulling you into a direction that everyone calls normal, everyone calls necessary, everyone calls the way of men. Later, when you are older and you have learned to name things, you realize it was not the earth. It was people. It was the fear of being laughed at. It was the hunger to be accepted. It was the wish to be counted as one of the real ones.

I did not wake up one morning and say, "Today I will change my face forever." I was pulled into it slowly, the way a river pulls a child who thinks he is only washing his feet at the edge. It began with the talk of boys, the kind of talk that is half joking and half serious. It began with the way older boys look at you, not with hatred, but with that cold measuring that tells you, without words, that you are still outside. It began with the names that separate you from them, the words that place you in the category of children, even when your body is growing and your mind is already carrying heavy thoughts.

In our world, the face is not only a face. It is a statement. It is a public record. It is a passport that your community reads quickly, without asking you questions. When the marks are there, people do not ask if you are ready. They assume you are ready. They begin to speak to you differently. They begin to expect from you what they expect from a man. That change can feel like honor. It can also feel like a trap.

My father, Maluth Abiel Kueth, warned me. He did not warn me as a man who hated culture. He warned me as a man who understood life and understood regret. He told me not to do it. He told me that the scars were not needed for me to become a man. But I did not listen. I did what many boys do when they are standing between a father's wisdom and a crowd's laughter. I chose the crowd. I chose the immediate safety of belonging. I chose the short relief of being accepted. I chose it, and then I carried it on my forehead for the rest of my life.

It is difficult to explain the power of peer pressure to someone who has never lived where community is not only social, but survival. In some places, you can be different and still be safe. In some places, you can refuse and still eat with others, still marry, still be treated as human. But in our setting, refusing can mean losing your place among age-mates. It can mean becoming the story that others use to teach fear. It can mean living inside a question mark where people keep asking, "What is wrong with him?" even when nothing is wrong with you.

When I remember that season of my life, I remember the faces of boys around me. Some of them are gone now. Life in our land can be brutal, and many do not reach old age. That is another painful layer of it. You can be pressured by people who are also pressured, boys who are also afraid, boys who are trying to prove something before war, hunger, disease, and accidents prove something else. You can bleed for belonging today, and tomorrow the same circle that mocked you will be reduced by death. That truth does not erase responsibility, but it makes the story heavier.

What did I think I was buying with those scars? I thought I was buying a name. I thought I was buying a shield against shame. I thought I was buying a place. I wanted to be seen as courageous. I wanted to be seen as qualified. I wanted to be addressed in the language of men, not in the language of boys. Later, I learned that courage that is demanded is not always courage. Sometimes it is fear wearing the clothes of bravery.

One of the first "benefits" I noticed after scarification was not internal. It was social. People began to separate me from boys. They began to treat me as a man, even when I was still learning how to carry myself as one. In the cultural logic of our communities, the marks signal transition. They are taken as proof that a boy has crossed a line, and once he has crossed it, the world adjusts its expectations.

That separation from boys is often praised as growth, and in some ways it can push you forward. A young man who is treated as a man begins to practice responsibility earlier. He begins to sit with older men and listen. He begins to be entrusted with tasks. He begins to be included in discussions where decisions are made. He begins to feel the weight of accountability. That can mature a person.

But there is also a shadow side that people do not say loudly. When you are separated from boys, you are also separated from softness. You are separated from the permission to fail openly. You are separated from the space where mistakes are forgiven as childish. Once you have the marks, your mistakes are no longer "boy mistakes." They are "man mistakes." And the punishment for "man mistakes" can be harsh, sometimes even when the mistake is simply being young.

I remember how quickly the language around me changed. The jokes changed. The insults changed. The expectations changed. Some people became warmer toward me, because I was now one of them. Others became more demanding, because I was now supposed to prove that the marks meant something. A face can become a promise. And when a face is a promise, every act becomes an examination.

This is where the weight of belonging becomes clear. Belonging is not free. Belonging has rules. Belonging is paid for with conformity. And in our setting, one of the most visible forms of conformity is what you carry on your skin.

People often speak about scarification as identity. That is true. The patterns can signal clan and community. They can tell stories without words. In times of conflict, such marks have been used to identify who is "ours" and who is not, which some see as a form of protection. But even that "protection" has two edges. If marks can identify a friend, they can also identify a target. If marks can protect you in one setting, they can expose you in another.

Then there are the physical realities that follow you quietly, long after the ceremony is finished and the songs have faded. The body remembers. The skin remembers. The risk is not only the pain you feel on the day of cutting. It is infection. It is scarring that can go wrong. It is the possibility of disease transmission when tools are not clean and procedures are not safe. Even when we speak carefully, we must say the truth: practices that involve cutting skin with shared or unsterilized instruments can carry serious risks, including bloodborne diseases.

When I was fifteen, I did not think in medical terms. I did not think of HIV. I did not think of Hepatitis B. I did not think of bacteria. I thought of laughter. I thought of status. I thought of the immediate social world in front of me. That is how many boys think. Not because they are foolish, but because survival at that age is often social survival.

A boy who is isolated can become vulnerable in ways he cannot explain. So he chooses what looks like safety, even if it is risky.

The consequences are not only physical. They are also psychological. There is a kind of inner conflict that grows when you realize you did something permanent for reasons that were temporary. The pressure to conform can create resentment, especially when you later see that the same community that demanded your conformity is not always gentle with you afterward. Some people live with pride in their scars. Others live with quiet regret. Some live with both at once, pride on some days, regret on others.

I have carried both, at different times.

I have also learned that not everyone experiences the marks in the same way. Some people celebrate them fully. Some people wish they could erase them. I have heard men speak openly about wanting to remove their scars even when the scars are not as visible as others. That honesty matters, because it breaks the myth that scarification is universally desired by everyone who has it.

When we pretend that every bearer is proud, we silence those who are not. And when we silence those who are not, we make it harder for the next generation to choose wisely. Silence is one of the tools that keeps harmful pressure alive.

Another consequence is the way scarification can divide people. It is supposed to unite, but it can also separate. It can create categories of "real" and "not real." It can produce discrimination against those who do not have the marks. It can make a person feel excluded for refusing. This exclusion can cut deeper than the scars themselves, because it attacks dignity and self-worth.

I have watched how these categories play out in conversations, in jokes, in marriage discussions, and in community arguments. The marks can become a weapon used to belittle others. And once a tradition becomes a weapon, it stops being only tradition. It becomes control.

That is why, as I grew older, the story on my forehead stopped being only about what happened when I was fifteen. It became about how communities shape choices, and how choices shape lives. It became about the responsibility of elders to guide boys well, not only to preserve culture, but to protect life. It became about the responsibility of boys, too, to learn to say no, even when no is hard.

But saying no is not a simple moral sentence in our setting. It requires a supportive environment. It requires elders who defend the boy who refuses. It requires a community that understands that manhood is bigger than scars. And that is not always available.

If I could speak to my younger self, I would not only say, "Do not do it." I would also say, "You are already a man in the making even without it." I would say, "The crowd is not your judge." I would say, "Your father's voice is not weakness." I would say, "A clean forehead is not shame." But young ears do not always hear what older mouths speak. They hear what their age-mates repeat. They hear what laughter teaches. They hear what fear demands.

And still, I must also tell the full truth. There were moments when the scars did help me socially. There were moments when I was treated with a kind of respect that I might not have received otherwise. There were doors of acceptance that opened. There were times when being marked meant being counted.

That is why this issue is not black and white. It carries both advantage and harm. It carries both pride and regret. It carries both identity and risk.

But even when we admit the advantages, we must ask the harder questions.

Should belonging require blood?

Should identity require pain?

Should a boy be pushed into permanence before he understands permanence?

Should a father's counsel be defeated by laughter?

Those questions live with me because I know what it means to be fifteen and to feel that your entire future depends on whether you are accepted today. I also know what it means to be older and to realize that the future is long, and the face is always with you.

There is another consequence that people do not always discuss openly, especially in cultures that praise toughness. It is the way scarification can train a boy to associate manhood with silence. In many ceremonies, the ability to endure pain without crying is praised. Composure becomes a badge. That can build resilience, yes. But it can also teach emotional suppression. It can teach a boy that expressing pain is shameful. And later, when that boy becomes a man facing war, loss, and hardship, he may carry that training into adulthood in unhealthy ways.

A community needs strong men, but strong does not have to mean emotionally dead.

I have thought about this especially because scarification is often tied to other expectations. Once marked, a boy is expected to act brave in everything, to fight, to defend cattle, to endure hunger, to walk long distances without complaint, to be the kind of man the community can rely on during crisis. Some of these expectations create admirable discipline. Others can crush a young person's inner life if there is no balance.

The physical mark becomes a symbol that the community reads as "ready." But readiness is not carved by a blade alone. Readiness is built by guidance, teaching, and time.

As time went on, I began to see that culture is not a stone. It is alive. It changes, even when people pretend it does not. Some communities have already reduced scarification. Some have stopped it. Some have tried to make it safer. Some have tried to replace it with other forms of identity expression. People debate these things fiercely, because culture is tied to dignity. When a practice changes, some feel they are losing themselves. Others feel they are finally protecting themselves.

I stand in the middle, because I understand both sides.

I understand the desire to preserve identity. I understand the pride that comes from carrying a symbol that connects you to ancestors and age-sets and shared history. I understand why some people call these marks "writing," as if the face is a page. I also understand the health risks, the social coercion, and the lifelong regret that can follow a decision made under pressure.

If we are serious about the future, we must learn how to honor heritage without harming the body and the mind. That requires open talk, not threats. It requires education, not mockery. It requires communities that can say, "We will still count you as ours even if you choose differently."

And it also requires personal honesty.

My honesty is this: I wish I had listened to my father. I love my people, and I respect where we come from. But I also know that some cultural practices are carried forward more by fear of shame than by true meaning. When meaning is replaced by fear, the practice becomes a chain.

The scars on my forehead have been many things to me across the years. They have been a badge in one season, a regret in another, a lesson in another. They have made me think deeply about how communities form identity, how boys become men, and how easily people can be pressured into choices they cannot undo.

This chapter is not only about the scars. It is about belonging. It is about the cost of being accepted. It is about the heavy truth that the desire for a good name can push a young person into decisions that shape the rest of his life. It is about the way we should protect the next generation from the worst side of our own expectations.

Because if we do not, we will continue to produce men who wear cultural pride on their skin but carry cultural wounds in their hearts.

And we will keep calling it tradition, when sometimes it is simply fear.

If you are a young person reading this, I will not insult you by pretending the pressure is small. It is real. But I will tell you something simple that I had not fully learned at fifteen.

You can belong without bleeding.

You can be a man without being cut.

And if the people around you refuse to see that, then the problem is not your face.

The problem is the kind of belonging they are offering.

CHAPTER 4: THE IDEA OF MARKS

Before I ever lay down for the cuts, the marks already existed in my mind as an idea. That idea was larger than skin. It was larger than pain. It was larger than the ceremony itself. It was a story I had heard and absorbed long before I understood myself well enough to question it.

In many communities like mine, facial marks are not treated as decoration. They are treated as a language. They speak without your permission. They announce something about where you come from, what stage of life you have entered, and what your community expects from you. The marks can be read as emblems of maturity, respect, and cultural identity. That is not just a poetic sentence. It is the reality of how people respond when they see you. A marked face is often assumed to be a responsible face. A marked face is often assumed to be a face that has endured.

That is why, when boys discuss scarification, they rarely speak first about health or long-term cost. They speak about meaning. They speak about honor. They speak about identity. They speak about belonging. They speak about the way elders treat those who have crossed that line. They speak about the way age-mates stop calling you a child and begin calling you a man.

The idea of marks is often tied to age-sets.

In the place where I later spent time and learned more, the Ngok Lual Yak Dinka, age-sets shape social life in serious ways. The text in this book describes age-sets as fundamental, and it even names a concluding age-set, Ayaau, marked by the absence of scarification. That detail is important because it shows something many outsiders miss. Scarification is not always the only anchor of identity. Age-sets can continue even when scarification is absent. Social structure can remain even when physical marking changes.

Yet, next to that example, the same text observes that scarification remains a life-stage marker for the Nuer, and it highlights how different communities express the idea of age-sets in different ways. That is exactly the point. The idea behind the marks often survives even when the marks differ, or even when marks disappear.

So, what is that idea?

At its simplest, the idea is that life has stages, and those stages need recognition. Childhood ends. Adulthood begins. Responsibility increases. Privileges change. The community wants a visible sign that a person has crossed into a new place. That is why scarification appears in many places as a marker of rites of passage.

But the idea goes deeper than a simple sign.

It is also about memory. When a community has limited written records, the body becomes a kind of record. The same document explains that investigating origins is difficult because early written records are limited, and that elders' accounts can be incomplete. In settings like that, the living body becomes a library. The face becomes a page. It carries what cannot be stored in books easily. It carries what is learned through repetition and oral teaching.

That does not mean every mark is wise. It does not mean every practice is safe. It does not mean every reason is pure. But it explains why the practice holds such emotional power. When you challenge scarification, some people feel you are challenging more than a practice. They feel you are challenging the community's memory and dignity.

This is why debates can become heated. The document itself says that the topic of facial scarification in South Sudan has long been a source of heated debates between those who defend it as cultural heritage and those who denounce it for health and human rights concerns. When a practice is tied to identity, people do not argue calmly. They argue as if their name is on trial.

I understand that, because at fifteen I was not thinking like a medical officer or a human-rights advocate. I was thinking like a boy who wanted to belong. The marks were not a public policy question to me. They were a personal identity question.

The idea of marks is also tied to the role of those who make them.

Scarification, in many communities, is not done by just anyone. It is done by specialized practitioners, and that specialization itself increases the sacredness of the act. The text describes skilled artisans known as

28

Gäär or Gëër who execute facial scarification, and it emphasizes that they carry traditional designs and techniques, applying patterns with care. It also says these practitioners often learn their craft from their fathers, passing knowledge through generations.

That matters for two reasons.

First, it shows that scarification is not only a boy's test. It is also a community's craft. There is a whole training system behind it, and people respect that system. They respect the Gäär because his hand can bring honor or shame. His hand can create a clean pattern or a ruined face. His hand can mean quick healing or prolonged suffering. His hand can mean controlled bleeding or dangerous blood loss. Even when people do not speak openly about these risks, everyone knows, deep down, that the one holding the tool carries power.

Second, it shows how tradition reproduces itself. Fathers teach sons. Sons become practitioners. Boys become men. Men become elders. The cycle continues. And when something becomes part of a cycle, it becomes hard to stop, because stopping it means disrupting a whole chain of roles, pride, and livelihood.

In this book, I do not present myself as the final authority on every tribe and every method. I am telling my story, and I am also looking at the wider picture as I learned it. That is why the earlier front matter of this book admits it is not a fully researched account, even though it draws on conversations and elders. I want to keep that honesty here too.

Still, even without claiming to know everything, I can say something with confidence. The idea of marks is not one idea only. It is a bundle of ideas living together.

One idea is beauty and craft.

When you look at the different ways communities mark the face, you see that people care deeply about precision. They care about symmetry. They care about arrangement. They care about neatness. The document gives a strong example in the Shilluk tradition. It explains that the Shilluk people use small aligned dots on the forehead, arranged in a continuous line. It calls attention to the care required, the steady hand, and the prestige of both practitioner and recipient.

The Shilluk example also adds something that should humble anyone who tries to reduce scarification to one narrow story. In that tradition, both boys and girls receive the dotted marks as part of initiation into adulthood. That is not a small detail. It shows how the meaning of marks can include gender equality in one community while taking a different shape in another. It also shows that the purpose is not always about men proving toughness. Sometimes it is simply a community's shared way of saying: you have crossed into responsibility.

Another idea is timing.

Scarification is often tied to prescribed ages, seasons, and community calendars. The document says the practice is often tied to specific tribes, seasons, and ages, guiding young people through transitions from one stage of life to another. This is part of what gives it power. It is not random. It is scheduled. It is expected. And when it is expected, refusing it can feel like refusing time itself, refusing the way the community measures growth.

Another idea is unity.

The document notes that elders sometimes step up to protect those who bear marks when they face discrimination or mistreatment, and it frames that intervention as a form of unity and solidarity. This is important because it shows something true. Even when scarification can be used to divide, it can also be used to unite. Elders defending marked youth is a sign that the community does not want its people humiliated for carrying a shared symbol.

But then the document also admits the hard side. It says people who opt against the practice can experience pressure, alienation, resentment, and tension inside communities. That is the side I know personally, even if I did not experience it as a refuser. I experienced it as someone pulled by the fear of that alienation. I could feel, even before the ceremony, that refusing would cost me social safety among age-mates.

So the idea of marks includes unity, but it also includes the threat of exclusion.

Another idea is difference, not as conflict, but as variety.

The text points out that marks vary between tribes in pattern and method, yet the underlying theme is similar: using scarification as a rite of passage. It also mentions other groups in Upper Nile such as the Mabaan and the Shilluk, stating that the importance of facial marks extends beyond one community. The Mabaan example says cheeks of boys and girls bear intricate markings at prescribed times of year, again tied to the transition into adulthood.

When you look at these examples together, you see the wider truth: the idea of marks is not just one tribe's practice. It is a wider African and human practice, expressed in many forms, shaped by geography, history, and social structure.

At the same time, the text warns that exploring origins is hard, due to limited written records. That means we should be careful when we claim certainty about who started what, or who influenced whom. People often say, "This practice came from that tribe," or "That one copied us," especially in places where conflict has sharpened identity politics. But if we are honest, many origin claims are difficult to prove fully, and elders' memories, while valuable, can be partial.

So, for me, the idea of marks is less about proving who invented them, and more about understanding what they do inside a community.

And what they do is powerful.

They make the body into a sign.

They make the face into a message.

They make a private person into a public symbol.

This is also why some people react strongly when outsiders criticize the practice. Outsiders may speak about health, rights, and modernity, and they may have valid points. But to the community, the criticism can sound like: your identity is ugly, your history is backward, your ancestors were foolish. People do not hear the careful argument. They hear insult.

That is why any discussion about scarification must be careful. Even the document says the issue demands sensitivity and respect for diverse viewpoints, and it notes the need for open dialogue and education.

I agree with that, but I also want to add something personal.

The idea of marks becomes dangerous when it stops being a choice.

When it becomes coercion.

When it becomes a social tax a boy must pay in blood.

When it becomes a condition for dignity.

This is where the idea shifts from meaning to harm.

The document asks, "Is scarification important?" and then it frames the issue as complex, with varied views, including concerns about health risks. It also acknowledges the physical toll, saying the process can inflict pain, cause infections, and carry risks like transmission of HIV or Hepatitis B.

That is not an academic warning. That is life.

Once you say "blood," you must also say "disease." Once you say "shared tools," you must also say "risk." In some places, people have tried to reduce the risk through sterilization and disposable instruments. The document says modern sterilization methods can minimize danger, but it also admits that access and affordability can be difficult, and it suggests education, disposable instruments, and cleaning protocols.

Those lines show a practical path, but they also expose a deeper truth. The practice is often happening in communities where medical supplies and consistent health services are not guaranteed. So the idea of marks, in the modern world, is no longer only cultural. It has become a public health question too.

When I was fifteen, none of that was in my head in a clear way. What was in my head was the social meaning. I thought the marks were a doorway into respect. I thought they would raise me. I thought they would protect me from being treated as a boy. The danger felt distant.

But pain has a way of bringing distant danger close.

And in my own story, danger did come close, through blood loss. In another part of this book, I wrote about bleeding heavily, appearing lifeless, and being unable to respond to questions. That moment is not separate from this chapter because it proves something. It proves that the idea of marks can be romantic, but the body is real. The body bleeds. The body can fail. The body can be harmed by what the mind celebrates.

So, the idea of marks must be held with two hands.

One hand holds meaning.

The other holds risk.

One hand holds identity.

The other holds cost.

One hand holds heritage.

The other holds health.

And if we hold only one hand, we lie.

Some people try to hold only meaning and deny risk. Others try to hold only risk and deny meaning. Both sides create more conflict because they refuse to see what the other side sees.

This is where I stand, as a person who has the marks.

I cannot pretend the marks mean nothing. They shaped how people saw me. They shaped how I saw myself. They shaped my place among my age-mates. They shaped my memory of my father's refusal. They shaped my later thinking about pressure and choice.

But I also cannot pretend the marks are harmless. They are born from pain. They carry health risks. They can be forced by social pressure. They can divide communities. They can create discrimination, not only against those without marks, but sometimes even against those with marks, especially when outsiders misunderstand the symbol.

This is why, when I revisit the idea of marks, I do not see only a cultural badge. I see a human story.

I see a boy trying to become someone.

I see elders trying to preserve a way of life.

I see communities trying to maintain order through rites and visible signs.

I see the craft of the Gäär, learned from fathers, passed down through generations.

I see the beauty of careful patterns, like the Shilluk dots aligned with precision.

I also see the risk of infection, disease transmission, and harm.

And I see the weight of community expectation, the pressure that can turn a rite into a trap.

The biggest danger of the idea of marks is not the marks themselves. The biggest danger is when the marks become a substitute for real maturity.

A boy can be marked and still be childish inside.

A boy can endure pain and still be unable to endure responsibility.

A boy can pass a test of silence and still fail the test of character.

A community can mark people and still fail to raise them well.

In that sense, scarification can be a powerful symbol, but a symbol is not the same thing as the substance it claims to represent.

This is where I think the conversation must go, especially for our generation.

The document suggests seeking alternatives, such as less invasive forms of body modification like tattoos or piercings, as ways to express cultural pride without the same risks. Some people will reject that idea completely, because they will say it is not ours. Others will accept it, because they will say survival matters more than preserving a method. I am not writing this chapter to force everyone into one answer. I am writing it to open a door for honest thinking.

Because the truth is, even traditions change.

The document itself says traditions are living entities that evolve with changing circumstances and needs. That is a hard sentence for many people, because it sounds like betrayal. But it is also a true sentence. Nothing human stays frozen. Even when people defend a practice passionately, the practice has already changed in many ways across time, across tribes, across geography, across tools, and across the influence of modern education and health awareness.

So, what should remain constant if methods change?

The meaning.

If scarification is meant to mark maturity, then the core should be maturity.

If it is meant to mark responsibility, then the core should be responsibility.

If it is meant to mark belonging, then the core should be belonging without humiliation and coercion.

If it is meant to honor heritage, then the core should be honoring heritage without creating unnecessary suffering.

That is how I now understand the idea of marks.

Not as a simple yes or no.

Not as a simple pride or shame.

But as a question that needs both respect and courage.

Respect, because people's identity is not a joke.

Courage, because people's health and freedom are not a joke either.

When I was fifteen, I did not have the tools to think this way. I was not weighing arguments. I was not studying health risks. I was not asking what belongs to me as choice and what belongs to me as pressure. I was doing what boys do when the community offers one loud path to acceptance.

Now, with age, the marks have become a teacher.

They have taught me that a community can give you meaning, but it can also demand too much from you.

They have taught me that the body is not a playground for social approval.

They have taught me that identity should never be built on fear of mockery.

They have taught me that cultural pride is good, but it must not become cultural cruelty.

They have taught me that even when elders defend a tradition, they should also defend the freedom of a young person to choose.

Because a tradition that cannot survive choice will only survive through force, and anything that survives through force will eventually create resentment.

So this chapter ends where it began.

The marks were an idea before they were a cut.

They were a story before they were blood.

They were belonging before they were pain.

And because they are an idea, not only a wound, we can talk about them honestly.

We can ask what they have given us.

We can ask what they have taken from us.

We can ask whether the same meaning can be carried with less harm.

We can ask whether we are preserving heritage or preserving pressure.

We can ask whether a boy should be cut to prove he belongs, or whether belonging should be given first, and the boy allowed to grow into the community through responsibility and character.

That is what the idea of marks has become for me now.

Not just the lines on my forehead.

But the questions those lines keep asking me every time I look in the mirror.

PART II
CHAPTER 5: THE WINTER DECISION

I was fifteen when I chose the marks.

That sentence sounds clean when I write it now, as if it was a calm decision made with a clear head and a steady heart. It was not. It was a storm made of voices. Some voices were outside me, from boys my age and older boys who had already crossed that line. Some voices were inside me, the ones that wanted a name, a place, and a face that could not be questioned.

In our world, a boy's face was not only a face. It could be a declaration. It could be a passport. It could be a wall. It could be a welcome. A forehead could be a story that everyone could read, even people who had never met you. That is what the marks were supposed to do. They were meant to say: this one belongs. This one endured. This one is counted.

Yet in my own house, the clearest voice was my father's, and it was against it. He advised me not to receive scarification marks on my forehead, but I still went for them, and later I had to live with the truth that I did not follow his counsel.

That is where the trouble begins, because when a father speaks in our setting, he does not speak as a random man giving an opinion. He speaks as the one who carried your name before you, as the one who knows the community's winds, as the one who has seen boys bleed and heal and still end up regretting it. When he warns you, he is not trying to make you small. He is trying to keep you whole.

But a boy of fifteen can be a strange creature. He can fear pain, yet chase it. He can love his father, yet rebel against the very hand that fed him. He can be wise in some things and foolish in the very thing that will stay with him for the rest of his life. I was that boy.

I had grown up watching the older ones. In our society, there is always a ladder, even if nobody calls it a ladder. There are those who have crossed and those who have not. There are those who can speak and those who must listen. There are those who can sit with men and those who remain at the edge of the circle. A boy without marks could still be brave, still be good, still be intelligent, but he would always have to explain himself. And explanations are tiring, especially when you are young and you want a straight road, not a debate.

I also carried something else that many young boys carry, even if they do not confess it. I wanted a good name. I wanted to be seen as someone who would not shrink when the hard thing arrived. I wanted to stand in front of my age-mates without feeling like I was borrowing courage from someone else. That desire for standing and recognition was one of the forces behind my choice.

Still, desire alone does not cut skin. A whole season of pressure prepares the blade.

The timing matters. Scarification was often done in winter, and there were reasons for that, reasons people could explain with the language of weather, healing, and careful care. Cooler temperatures reduce swelling. Dry air can make wound care easier. The season also gathers people, and the ceremony becomes a communal event, not a private act.

But winter also brings its own rules. Boys healing from scarification were often isolated, housed in special places, protected from contamination, and kept away from certain contacts that people believed could slow healing, including contact with cattle or women. That separation was not only medical. It was social. It was a way of saying: these ones are in passage. Do not disturb their crossing.

Even the names for boys in that stage show the weight given to the season. In Dinka and Nuer cultures, boys undergoing that coming of age ritual were called "cɔ̈t" or "cɔat." The words are short, but they carry the meaning of being in between, no longer fully a child, not yet fully a man, but already marked by the intention to become one.

So winter came, and with it came talk.

Talk around fires. Talk in the cattle camps. Talk during walks. Talk during the small pauses of life when boys gather and test one another's hearts with jokes that are not jokes. Talk that asks, without asking, "Are you one of us yet?"

And in that talk, a boy learns that courage is not only the ability to endure pain. Courage is also the ability to refuse. That second courage is rarer. It is easier to endure the knife than to endure the laughter of your age-mates. It is easier to bleed once than to bleed slowly through shame.

I will not pretend I was a hero of refusal. I was pulled by the same currents that pull many boys. A boy wants to belong. A boy wants to avoid the feeling that he is being left behind. A boy wants to look like the others so he can stop being a question.

When I look back now, I can see the pattern clearly. The pressure does not arrive in one day. It arrives in small daily waves. First it is a joke. Then it is a nickname. Then it is a story told loudly about another boy who delayed and later regretted it. Then it is the silent change in how certain people treat you, especially those who already have the marks. They do not even need to insult you. They only need to stop including you in certain conversations. Exclusion can speak louder than mockery.

At home, my father's warning remained steady. He had his reasons, and I respect them even more now because he was not speaking from ignorance. He was speaking from knowledge of consequences.

Yet my life at that time was not only my home. It was also my age group. It was also the community. It was also the hidden court of teenage opinion where boys judge boys for things that they themselves do not fully understand. In that court, the sentence for refusing can feel heavier than the pain of the blade.

Once the decision starts forming, the world begins preparing you without asking your permission.

You notice the artisans more.

In our cultures, the scarification is not done by just anyone. It is done by skilled men known as Gäär or Gëër, men who know the designs and the method, and who do not approach it like play. Many of them learn the craft from their fathers, passing it down like a trade, like a duty, like a guarded family skill.

To an outsider, it might look like cruelty. To those inside, it is a serious cultural act, carried by men who understand what can go wrong if the hand shakes or the blade is dull or the pattern is uneven. The Gäär does not only cut. He carries a community's expectation on his fingers.

Before the day itself, there is preparation, and not only of tools. There is preparation of the initiate's place, a resting place made for him, a small sign that even though you are going to face pain, you are not being abandoned. The preparation for scarification includes creating a resting place for the boy, a symbol of care and support.

That detail matters to me, because it shows the mixed nature of the practice. It can harm, and it can also contain love. It can wound, and it can also gather a community around a boy so that he is not alone in the aftermath.

In the days leading up to it, the atmosphere around boys like me changes. People begin to look at you differently. Some look at you with pride before you have done anything. Some look at you with pity, because they know what is coming. Some look at you with expectation, as if you have already promised them you will not cry.

And you begin to rehearse in your mind how you will behave.

You rehearse not screaming. You rehearse not flinching. You rehearse being the kind of boy who can stare at the sky while pain is drawn onto his skin. You imagine the moment over and over, and sometimes you imagine it as if it is a victory, and sometimes you imagine it as if it is your death.

I had heard stories about bleeding. Everyone had.

Bleeding was not a side detail. It was part of the reality. Some boys bled more than others. Some lost so much blood that people panicked. In my own experience, the blood loss became severe, and I appeared lifeless to onlookers, unable to respond to them. I did not know that would be my story, but even before it happened, I knew bleeding was not a joke.

There was also a practical detail that many people outside our communities would never imagine: during the procedure, a shallow pit was dug near the back of the boy's head to collect blood. The boy lay facing down, eyes turned up, exposed to the sky. That image stayed in my mind even before I lived it. It is one thing to hear "you will bleed." It is another to picture a pit made for your blood.

In my mind, I tried to control the future by thinking about it. I told myself, if I picture it enough, then when it happens it will not surprise me. That was my teenage attempt at wisdom. I thought preparation of the mind could cancel shock. I did not yet understand that the body has its own language, and pain speaks that language fluently.

As winter advanced, the social temperature rose.

There were boys who had already gone through it, and they walked differently, not because they were better humans, but because the community treated them as if they had passed a gate. When they spoke, their words carried weight that a boy without marks could not easily carry. Even silence from them could feel like a message.

Some boys would show their scars like trophies. Some would touch them absent-mindedly while talking, not to show off, but because the scars had become part of their face, like a new muscle memory. And there were those who would exaggerate their bravery, telling stories of how they did not even feel pain, as if pain is something you can defeat by lying about it.

I listened to all of it.

I also watched how girls and women looked at the marked boys. Not every look was admiration, but enough of those looks existed to feed a teenage boy's hunger for being seen. A boy notices what the community praises, and he tries to become the praised thing.

At the same time, my father's warning stood like a wall inside me. It was not loud like the boys' jokes. It was not dramatic. It was steady. That steadiness is sometimes the hardest thing to fight, because you cannot dismiss it as noise. You cannot call it childish. You cannot blame it on youth.

So I began doing what many young people do when they are about to disobey a parent. I began gathering reasons. I began building a defense in my mind.

I told myself that scarification was about identity. I told myself it was about belonging. I told myself that the community had survived through these practices, and who was I to reject what held us together?

I also told myself that I would be fine. I told myself that thousands of boys had done it. I told myself that the pain would pass. I told myself that it was only a moment compared to a lifetime of being questioned.

Those reasons sounded strong at night. In the morning, they sounded weaker. But by then, I had already stepped into the current, and currents do not easily release those who enter them willingly.

The days before the ceremony were filled with small rituals that were not officially called rituals.

You begin to eat differently. You begin to sleep differently. You begin to pay attention to your body as if it is about to become someone else's project. You begin to feel your forehead as if it is already marked. You begin to imagine the lines.

You also begin to notice how elders speak about the Gäär. They speak with respect. They speak as if the Gäär carries not only a blade but also a kind of authority. And it makes sense, because if the Gäär makes a mistake, the mistake becomes permanent. A wrong cut does not vanish. It stays on your face like a sentence.

The Gäär, in that sense, is both artist and judge. He must cut cleanly, with accuracy. He must do it with tradition, not invention. The community expects the marks to look like what they have always looked like, because the pattern is not just decoration. It is a sign.

In my childhood mind, I imagined the Gäär as a man without fear. I imagined him as someone who could cut without feeling anything. Later I understood that the Gäär also carries pressure, because a trembling hand can ruin a face. Whether he admits it or not, he too is watched.

On the eve of the day, the world becomes quiet in a particular way.

People do not necessarily stop talking, but the jokes soften. The teasing becomes less sharp. Even boys who pushed you into the decision begin to treat you as someone who is about to suffer, and suffering, even when culturally accepted, tends to silence mockery for a while.

You sense that something serious is approaching.

And in that quiet, doubt tries to speak.

I remember moments when I wanted to step back. I remember moments when the idea of my father's eyes on me felt heavier than all the voices outside. I remember moments when I wondered if I was being foolish.

But the trap with certain cultural steps is this: once you have signaled readiness, stepping back becomes another kind of shame. It can look like fear. It can look like weakness. And for a fifteen-year-old boy, being seen as weak can feel like being erased.

So I continued forward.

Then came the morning.

Winter mornings in our environment have a particular bite. The air is cold enough to make your skin tighten. Your breath appears. The grass holds a kind of quiet wetness, yet the larger world feels dry. People move with purpose. Fires burn. Smoke rises. The sky looks like it is watching.

It is strange how, on such days, ordinary things become intense.

A small bowl becomes important. Water becomes important. Cloth becomes important. Even the ground becomes important, because you will lie on it.

And the resting place, prepared for the boy, becomes a center point, a small sign that you will not just be cut and left.

There is also the gathering. Scarification is not something done in secret. It is an event. It carries the weight of community witness. The communal nature of the ceremony is part of what gives it power.

I was not the only one. Other boys were there. Some were more excited. Some were more quiet. Some looked like they wanted to vomit but were forcing their faces to remain calm.

44

When you are among boys about to be scarified, you see different types of courage.

There is the loud courage that talks too much, laughing too hard, trying to use noise to hide fear. There is the silent courage that avoids eye contact, saving energy. There is the spiritual courage that whispers prayers. There is the stubborn courage that refuses to imagine failure.

And then there is the courage that does not exist yet, but will be forced into existence once the blade touches skin.

As the moment approached, I became aware of my own body in a new way. My forehead felt too exposed. My skin felt too thin. My heart felt like it was beating against my ribs like it wanted to escape.

I also became aware of the sky.

That might sound like a poetic detail, but it is also literal. In the process, the boy lies prone, and his gaze is fixed upward, toward the heavens. Even before I lay down, I knew that was how it would be. I had heard it described. I had pictured it. Now it was becoming real.

Then came the practical act that made everything unmistakably real: the digging of the shallow pit near the back of the boy's head, meant to collect the blood.

When you see a pit being dug for your blood, your mind cannot pretend anymore. This is not a story. This is not a dare. This is not a joke between boys. This is flesh, blood, and permanence.

I wish I could say that at that moment I stood up and walked away, choosing my father's wisdom over my age group's expectations. But I did not.

Instead, I did what many boys do when they are trapped between love and pride. I went forward with a tight throat and a heart that was trying to be brave.

In those final minutes before the first cut, time behaves strangely.

A second becomes long. A sound becomes sharp. A glance from an elder becomes heavy. Even the movement of the Gäär's hands becomes something you watch like you are watching your own life being rearranged.

And somewhere inside that tense silence, I felt the strange mixture that would define much of my youth: the desire to become someone respected, and the fear that I might be paying too high a price for respect.

I also felt the absence of my father's approval like a shadow.

He had warned me. In my mind, I tried to push that thought away, but it returned again and again. The problem with true advice is that it does not disappear when you ignore it. It waits for you on the other side.

As the Gäär came closer, as the tools were readied, as the community settled into the posture of watching, I realized something that I had not fully admitted until then.

No matter how much we talk about culture, the cut is always personal.

Every boy faces the blade alone, even if a crowd surrounds him. Even if people sing. Even if people encourage him. Even if the community will later celebrate his new face. In the moment of cutting, there is only your skin, the blade, and the thin line between holding yourself and losing yourself.

I did not know how much I would bleed. I did not know that I would later appear lifeless and fail to answer people's questions. I did not know that the pit meant to collect blood would soon hold more than a child should lose.

All I knew then was that the moment had arrived.

The winter air was still.

The ground was ready.

The pit was waiting.

And the Gäär, trained in this craft, stood prepared to write a story on my forehead with a blade, the way our communities have long treated scars as a form of inscription and identity.

I looked up at the sky, because that is what a boy does when he is about to be cut, and because at fifteen, sometimes the sky feels like the only witness who cannot mock you.

Then I lay down.

CHAPTER 6: SILENCE UNDER THE KNIFE

When people speak about scarification, they often speak about it as if it is one thing, one moment, one test of bravery, and then it is done. But for the boy lying there, it is not one thing. It is a chain of moments, each one carrying its own fear, its own meaning, and its own demand. The day of the cut is not only the day of the cut. It is the day when all the talk becomes real, and the body is asked to keep promises that the mouth made too easily.

I remember the morning with a kind of sharpness that surprises me even now. Some memories fade into a general picture, but this one stays vivid. It stays vivid because the body remembers what the mind wants to forget. It stays vivid because the skin was changed, and the skin does not forget its own history.

Before the first cut, there was preparation.

In our communities, preparation is not treated as an optional detail. It is treated as part of the rite. A comfortable resting place is made for the initiate, and that resting place is not just a mat or a spot on the ground. It is a statement that the community is not throwing you into pain and abandoning you. It is a visible sign of care and support.

At fifteen, I did not sit and analyze these signs the way I can now. I only felt them. I felt that I was being moved from ordinary life into a special space, a space where everything would revolve around the cut and the healing. That shift alone can make a boy feel important. It can also make him feel trapped, because once you are placed in that special space, the community has already declared, without asking your heart again, that you will go through with it.

The resting place also carries another meaning that is not always spoken. It says, your pain will be witnessed. It says, your blood will not fall into the dust like the blood of a forgotten animal. It says, people will watch you, and watching can be both comfort and pressure.

The other part of preparation is mental, and our culture has a strict expectation about the mind on that day. Maintaining silence and composure during the procedure is treated as vital. It is tied to self-control and respect for the tradition. This expectation is one of the strongest social forces in the entire rite.

You can be afraid. People accept that you will be afraid. But they do not accept that you will show it.

You can feel pain. People accept that you will feel pain. But they do not accept that you will cry like a child.

The boy is expected to become a statue of discipline, even when his blood is leaving him. That expectation is why I say the ceremony is not only about scars. It is also about training. It trains the body to obey the community's image of manhood. It trains the face to hide the inner storm.

I had rehearsed that silence in my mind before the day came. I had told myself I would not shout. I had told myself I would not beg. I had told myself I would not give my age-mates a story that would follow me for years. But rehearsing is one thing. The blade is another.

The scarification ceremony, as I described it later, is a communal event. It reinforces social bonds, celebrates the transition into manhood, and becomes a time for stories, camaraderie, and reaffirmation of cultural values. This is important, because it means you do not suffer alone. But it also means you do not suffer privately. Many eyes are there, and eyes can feel heavy.

When a crowd gathers for a ceremony like this, it carries many emotions at once. Some people are proud. Some are excited. Some are curious. Some are anxious. Some are simply there because it is what people do. The boy at the center of it feels those emotions around him like heat.

I remember how the atmosphere shifted once it was clear that it was time.

There was talk at first, the normal talk of people gathering, the normal laughter that tries to make the fear smaller. But as the procedure approached, the talk reduced, and a certain seriousness entered the air. It is a seriousness that does not need a speech. Everyone understands what is about to happen.

I was one of the young men being initiated. In the Dinka and Nuer cultures, boys in this stage have names that mark the stage itself. "cöt" and "cɔat" are words used for boys undergoing that coming-of-age ceremony, and the centerpiece of that ritual is forehead scarification. Even if I did not think of the label in that moment, the community thought of me as that. I was no longer only John. I was an initiate, a boy in transition.

The fact that winter was chosen for the ceremony was not random. People have long observed that cooler temperatures reduce swelling and inflammation, and that winter dryness can make wound care easier. I did not know these reasons in scientific language at fifteen, but I knew winter was the season for it, and I knew the community had its wisdom about why.

Winter also came with isolation after the marks. Young men undergoing scarification are often housed in designated spaces during winter to protect healing wounds from contamination. There is also a widespread belief that contact with cattle or women can hinder healing, and so strict separation is enforced. All of that was already waiting on the other side of the blade. Even before the first cut, the ritual was beginning to rearrange my life.

Still, all of that was future. The present was the ground, the air, the eyes of people, and the reality of what the blade would do.

In the telling of my own story, bleeding is one of the central memories, not as an abstract warning, but as something that happened to me. I experienced severe blood loss following the application of the marks, and because of the extent of the bleeding, I appeared lifeless to onlookers and could not respond to their questions. That sentence is simple on paper, but the moment itself was terrifying.

But before the blood came, there was the act that made blood inevitable.

The pit.

During the procedure, a shallow pit was excavated near the back of the boy's head to collect the blood. The child lay facing down, eyes fixed upward, exposed to the sky. The pit is a detail that is so raw that some people might think it is exaggerated. It is not. It is part of the procedure, and it exists because everyone knows blood will flow.

When I saw that pit being made, something in me tightened. It was as if my body understood what my pride had been denying. It was not a game. It was not a rumor. It was not an argument with my father. It was blood.

Even then, I did not stand up.

That is one of the facts that still troubles me sometimes. A boy can see danger clearly and still move forward because the deeper danger for him is social humiliation. At fifteen, I feared the laughter of my peers more than I feared the possibility of serious harm. That is a hard thing to confess, but honesty is the only way to tell this story.

Peer pressure played a strong role in my decision. My father refused to consent to the ritual, but I remained fixed in my resolve, driven by the desire to fit in. Even now, when I read those words in my own earlier writing, I can feel the stubbornness of that boy. I can feel the pride. I can feel the hunger. I can feel the foolish courage that wanted to win a social battle at any cost.

The community around me had its own reasons for valuing the marks. The marks symbolize courage, resilience, and connection to the community. Those symbols are not imaginary. They shape how people treat you. They shape your sense of worth. In a world where many things are unstable, a stable symbol can feel like safety.

But the body does not care about symbols when the blade touches skin.

When it was time, I remember being positioned.

The posture itself is part of the humiliation and part of the sacrifice. You lie prone. Your face is turned upward. It feels strange, because your forehead is the target, yet your eyes are aimed at the sky. That posture forces you to accept what is happening without the comfort of seeing it clearly. You can hear the movement. You can sense the presence. You can feel the hands. But you cannot watch the blade the way you might want to, if you were trying to control the fear with your eyes.

And then, silence becomes the first test.

Not silence from the crowd only, but silence in you.

The expectation to maintain composure and self-control is not a small cultural preference. It is a central requirement. It is the rule that turns pain into a performance of manhood. It is the rule that makes the boy's face not only a place of scars, but also a stage where discipline is judged.

I remember the first touch of the tool and the first cut as a shock that spread through my whole body.

People who have never experienced such cutting might think it is like a quick injury that ends quickly. It is not. It is repeated. It is deliberate. It is measured. The practitioner is not making one cut. He is making a pattern. And the pattern must match what the community recognizes.

In my later reflections on the languages around scarification, I wrote that the Dinka and Nuer terms, such as gëër and gärị, carry a meaning close to writing, as if scarification is a form of inscription that marks identity and life stages. That is exactly what it feels like, except the ink is blood and the pen is a blade.

People call it writing, and in that moment, you realize why. Something is being written on you that you will carry into every conversation, every meeting, every photograph, and every mirror.

If the marks are writing, then pain is the language of the writing.

The cut burns, and the burn expands. It is not only the sharpness. It is also the heat of blood and skin reacting. It is your nerves screaming, and your pride ordering you to remain quiet.

I do not remember every sound I made, but I remember what mattered. I remember trying to keep my face steady. I remember trying to obey the rule of composure. I remember hearing some voices in the background, not necessarily mocking, but encouraging in the way

52

communities encourage someone they expect to endure. That encouragement can be love. It can also be pressure.

You do not want to disappoint them.

The strange thing is that the boy becomes responsible for everyone's pride. If he cries, people feel shame, not only for him but for the age-group and even for the families. This is why the text speaks about how actions and demeanor influence how others perceive not only the person but also the age-group and the community. This is not philosophy. It is social reality. A boy's reaction can become a story told for years.

That is why silence is such a heavy command.

So I tried to keep it.

But my body had its own truth.

The blood came fast.

At first, the blood is only something you sense, because the forehead is being cut, and you are lying in a posture that does not let you see the flow. But you can feel warmth. You can feel wetness. You can feel the heaviness of liquid leaving you. You can feel a strange weakness arriving.

Then the pit begins to do its job.

In my own account, I described how the pit collected so much blood that it reached the size of my adult hand, from fingertips to wrists. That image remains with me. It is one thing to hear a child bled a lot. It is another to picture the measurement with an adult hand, a hand that did not exist then, but exists now, used as a scale to measure what the child endured.

At fifteen, you do not know how to measure blood. You only know that something is leaving you, and your strength is decreasing.

I remember feeling a shift, a kind of coldness in my body that did not match the winter air. It was as if my life was moving outward into that pit. The body becomes light, but not in a good way. It becomes light like it is losing its anchor.

People around me noticed.

In my account, I wrote that because of the extent of the bleeding, I appeared lifeless to onlookers and could not respond to their questions. That is one of the most frightening parts, even now, because it means I was there, but not there. I was alive, but my body looked like death.

And there is a strange humiliation in that too, because a boy is trying to prove strength, and suddenly his body betrays him in front of everyone.

That is the moment when the community's pride can turn into fear.

This is also the moment when you realize that the ceremony is not fully in your control. A boy might think he can control whether he cries, whether he flinches, whether he shows weakness. But he cannot control how much he bleeds. He cannot control how his body reacts. He cannot control whether his blood pressure drops. He cannot control whether he faints.

In that sense, the ceremony strips you of the illusion that manhood is simply choice and bravery.

It shows you that life is fragile.

It shows you that a tradition can be meaningful and still be dangerous.

And it shows you that my father's refusal was not empty stubbornness. It was a protective instinct.

Even as I write this, I cannot escape the thought that my father's "no" was standing somewhere in the background of that scene, unseen but real. He did not consent, yet I went.

Sometimes, the clearest lesson of disobedience comes when the consequences become visible.

I am not trying to dramatize it. I am not trying to turn this into a story of near-death to make people admire me. I am telling it because it happened, and it shaped my thinking for years.

What is the feeling of appearing lifeless?

It is not romantic. It is not brave. It is a blur.

It is the sound of voices turning urgent.

It is the sense that people are around you and above you.

It is questions you cannot answer because your tongue is heavy and your mind is distant.

It is the frightening fact that you are still there, but your body is refusing to cooperate.

At that stage, courage becomes irrelevant. You cannot perform courage when you cannot respond.

All you can do is be carried by whatever care exists around you.

And care does exist.

For all the harshness of the ritual, communities do not want boys to die. This is part of why winter isolation and designated spaces exist, to protect wounds and speed healing. The community takes the healing stage seriously. The ritual is not only cutting. It is also the long care afterward.

Still, care does not erase the risk.

And risk is something I learned in my own body.

After the cutting and the bleeding, the world feels different.

You enter the stage of being separated, of being treated as fragile even though the marks were meant to signal strength. You are kept away from things believed to hinder healing. You are placed in that special space that was prepared.

This separation can feel like honor, because you are being protected and cared for. It can also feel like imprisonment, because your freedom is restricted and your body is in pain.

Pain after scarification is not only pain at the moment of cutting. It is pain that continues. The forehead throbs. The skin feels tight. The wound feels raw. And every movement of your face can remind you that you have been altered.

The community expects you to heal well. The healing is part of the success of the rite. In the cultural explanation, the healing process is eagerly anticipated and celebrated by the community, and a later celebration marks not only the completion of the ordeal but the entrance into a new life stage.

But healing is not only physical. There is also the inner adjustment.

You begin to sense that people are already treating you differently. They may speak to you as if you are older. They may include you in conversations you were excluded from before. They may call you by a different kind of name, a name that implies you are now among the men.

At fifteen, that change can feel like the reward for suffering.

It can also create a new pressure, because now you must live up to the image that the marks have created.

This is where the meaning of marks becomes complicated.

In my reflections, I wrote that the marks symbolize courage and resilience. That is the public meaning. But the private meaning can be different. The private meaning can include regret, fear, and a quiet anger at the pressure that pushed you there.

I do not say this to condemn my community. I say it to tell the truth about what happens inside a boy.

A boy can be proud and resentful at the same time.

A boy can feel honored and trapped at the same time.

A boy can feel that he has gained belonging and lost freedom at the same time.

When the blood had stopped and I was no longer in that lifeless state, I had time to think. Time in those isolated spaces is slow. It is slow

56

because you are not doing what you normally do. You are not running. You are not playing. You are not working the same way. You are waiting. You are healing.

And waiting is when regret sometimes starts speaking, quietly at first.

The first regret is not always regret about the marks themselves. Sometimes it is regret about why you did it.

You ask yourself, did I do this for meaning, or did I do it because I was afraid of being mocked?

For me, the answer was painful. Peer pressure drove me. And my father's refusal made that truth even sharper, because it meant I had rejected wisdom for approval.

This is also where I began to understand the phrase "good name" in a deeper way.

In my earlier writing, I admitted that from a young age I longed to earn a respected and honorable standing among my people, and that desire for a good name was a driving force, including in the decision to undergo scarification.

At fifteen, I thought a good name could be cut into a forehead.

Later, I learned a good name is built by how you live, not by how you bleed.

That is one of the lessons the scars kept teaching me long after the wounds healed.

During the healing stage, you become aware of how much of the ritual is about image.

You are expected to speak of it in certain ways.

You are expected to describe it as a victory.

You are expected to show gratitude for the tradition.

And even if you do feel gratitude, you might also feel something else that you do not easily speak.

I remember a strange personal disappointment that followed me for a while. It is not what most people expect. Many people think the only regret would be having scars at all. But my initial disappointment, as I admitted later, was about the size of my scars. I felt secretly disappointed that they were not as big as I had dreamed.

When I read that confession now, it almost makes me smile, not because it is funny, but because it shows how childish a boy can still be even after going through such a painful rite. I had just bled severely. I had appeared lifeless. And still, part of me was thinking, are the scars impressive enough?

That is how the desire for recognition can distort a mind.

It also shows something important. The rite is supposed to turn a boy into a man, but turning is not automatic. A ceremony can mark a moment. It cannot instantly mature the heart. The heart matures later, through life, through work, through losses, through responsibility, through reflection.

My disappointment about the size of the scars did not last forever. With time, I learned that the value of the scars was not in being grand. The value, if any value can be taken from them, was in the experiences and lessons they represented. I learned to see them as a reminder of endurance, and also as a reminder of the foolishness of peer pressure.

I do not want to pretend I became wise immediately after the ceremony. I did not. I was still young. But the experience planted something in me. It planted a seriousness about choices. It planted a suspicion of crowds. It planted a respect for my father's protective love.

I also began to look at the community's demands with a more careful eye.

The book I wrote earlier speaks about how the decision to undergo scarification should be personal, rooted in genuine connection to heritage rather than external pressure, and it warns of the consequences of succumbing to social pressure. That statement became real to me because I was the example of what happens when the pressure wins.

I also began to understand why the ceremony is surrounded by stories of ancestors and bravery. People tell these stories to strengthen the boy's heart, to make him believe he is joining a long line of heroic men. In itself, that can be inspiring. But it can also become a tool of coercion, because once you are told you are joining heroes, refusing feels like insulting your ancestors.

In the healing days, I had moments of pride too. I will not hide that. I felt that I had crossed a gate. I felt that I had survived. I felt that I had done what others expected. I felt relief, because the waiting and the fear were over.

But pride does not erase the memory of blood.

Pride does not erase the memory of appearing lifeless.

Pride does not erase the thought that this could have gone wrong in a final way.

And pride does not erase the face in the mirror.

One of the hardest truths about facial marks is that they do not give you the option of forgetting easily. A wound on the leg can be covered. A wound on the forehead is always present. Every time you meet someone new, the marks meet them before your words do. Every time you walk into a room, the marks enter with you.

That is why the mental adjustment after scarification can be long.

You begin to notice how people react.

Some react with respect.

Some react with curiosity.

Some react with assumptions.

Some react with fear, especially those who do not understand the practice and interpret the marks through their own stereotypes.

Even within our own communities, the marks can become a badge used to separate those who have them from those who do not. That separation can create pressure for others to conform, pressure that can become oppressive. This is why the book warns against excessive pressure that forces individuals into rigid conventions that clash with their convictions.

I had been one of the boys pushed by that pressure.

Now I was one of the marked ones, and I could see how easily a marked boy could become part of the machine that pressures others, simply by joining the mockery, simply by acting as if the marks are the only proof of manhood.

This is where a personal story becomes a moral question.

If I suffered because of pressure, will I pressure another?

If I bled for belonging, will I demand another boy bleed to belong?

If my father warned me, will I warn others, or will I laugh at them for refusing?

In those days, I did not frame it in these words, but the questions were there in a quieter form.

In the days of healing, the community's attention can be intense. People check on you. People talk about you. People evaluate how well you are healing. People judge whether the scars are forming well. People speak about the ceremony as if it is a public project, because in a way, it is.

And when you are fifteen, you feel exposed. Not only physically, but socially. Your pain is not only yours. Your healing is not only yours. Your face is now a public symbol.

Later, when I wrote about the linguistic meaning of scarification, I highlighted that the language itself treats scarification as inscription, a kind of writing that marks identity and life stages. That interpretation is not merely academic. It fits the lived experience. The community treats the scars as a text that can be read, and they feel invested in how that text looks.

This is why, even in my secret disappointment about scar size, I was thinking like someone living under that social reading. I wanted my "text" to look impressive. I wanted my "writing" to look like a strong statement.

But with time, I learned that the truest statement is not on the skin. It is in the life.

In reflecting on the aftermath, I cannot avoid another painful detail that always returns when I think of that season. Several companions who joined me in receiving the marks are no longer alive today, not because scarification killed them, but because our homeland has been torn by conflict, vengeance, and animosity that claimed their lives.

That line carries sorrow.

It carries the image of boys standing together, proving bravery to one another, only for later life to swallow them in larger storms. It carries the realization that the rites we treat as life-defining might not be the greatest dangers in our world. War, revenge, and instability have killed many, making the debates about scars both important and strangely small compared to the greater bleeding of the nation.

Yet, even if conflict is a bigger danger, it does not mean we should ignore avoidable harm.

A community already wounded by war should not add unnecessary wounds to its children.

That is one of the thoughts that grew in me as I matured.

Another thought that grew in me is about the kind of man I wanted to become.

At fifteen, I wanted a good name, and I thought scars could help.

After the ceremony, I began to see that a good name requires something different.

It requires character when nobody is watching.

It requires discipline in daily life, not only silence during a cut.

It requires respect for elders, including the elders whose counsel you do not like.

It requires the courage to stand alone sometimes.

It requires faith, for me personally, because I have often believed that God's guidance protected and guided me throughout my journey, and I have been thankful for that protection.

That belief did not begin only after scarification, but the experience gave it a new seriousness. When you feel your strength leaving you and you appear lifeless, you understand in your bones that life is not guaranteed. In such a moment, you either become humble, or you become hardened. I do not claim perfect humility, but I can say the experience pushed me toward gratitude.

In my later writing, I observed acquaintances who seemed to age quickly due to heavy drinking of "aregi," and I contrasted their deterioration with my own preserved youthfulness, which I attributed to divine guidance rather than my own wisdom. I mention that here because it connects to the same theme. Many young men chase proof of manhood through pain, drink, or reckless acts. But preservation of life often comes through restraint, not through excess.

That was another lesson I did not learn in one day, but scarification was one of the first major experiences that began shaping my thinking in that direction.

As my wounds healed, the scars began forming, and people began reacting to them as expected.

There is a moment, after the raw pain reduces, when the boy starts to believe he has truly crossed over. The community anticipates this healing and celebrates it. In some places, the celebration connects with the coming of a new year and the closing of the ordeal.

That celebration is not only for the boy. It is also for the community. It reaffirms who they are. It reminds them that their ways continue. It binds generations.

That is why people defend scarification passionately. They do not defend only a cut. They defend continuity.

Still, the personal story remains personal.

When I look back, I do not only remember the communal pride.

I remember the pit.

I remember the blood.

I remember my body failing to respond.

I remember the fear in people's voices.

I remember the fact that my father had refused.

And I remember how, even after surviving it, I was still a boy inside, disappointed that my scars were not as grand as I imagined.

Those mixed memories are part of why this book exists.

Because if I tell only the proud part, I lie.

And if I tell only the dangerous part, I also lie.

The truth is mixed, and life is mixed.

The chapter is called Silence Under the Knife because that silence was the test I faced first, and because silence is what the community values in that moment. But silence is also what kept me from speaking up before the ceremony, from telling my peers I did not truly want it, from saying I would rather keep my father's counsel.

In that sense, the silence began before the blade.

And the blade simply completed what silence had already allowed.

I think often about the kind of man my father was, and how he stood against the pressure, even though I did not listen. His refusal is one of the quiet pillars in my story. He was trying to protect me from exactly what happened. He could not stop me. But his warning did not vanish. It followed me.

It followed me into the pit.

It followed me into the blood loss.

It followed me into the healing days.

It followed me into the mirror.

And now it follows me into this book, because writing is also a form of scarification. Not on the skin, but on the page. It inscribes memory so that the next generation can read what we endured, and maybe choose differently where they can.

In the next chapter, I will continue from the healing stage into what it meant to carry those marks into life beyond the ceremony, into how the community treated me afterward, into how my own mind changed as years passed, and into how I began to see the marks not only as lines, but as a lifelong question.

CHAPTER 7: THE FACE THAT ENTERED THE WORLD FIRST

Healing is not a straight line. People talk about it as if it is one road from pain to health, from blood to strength, from boyhood to manhood. But when you are the one healing, it feels more like waves. One day you feel strong, the next day you feel weak again. One day you believe you made the right choice, the next day you wonder why you ever allowed it. One moment you feel honored, the next moment you feel trapped inside a decision that can never be undone.

After the blade, my life did not return to normal. It could not. The marks were on my forehead, and even if my wounds had closed in a week, the story they carried would last as long as my face lasted.

The first stage of healing was physical, but it was also social.

In our culture, the healing period is not treated as private recovery. It is treated as part of the rite itself. Winter, which is the season most associated with the ceremony, comes with special arrangements. Boys undergoing scarification are often housed in designated spaces to protect the healing wounds from contamination, and they are kept away from certain contacts that people believe can hinder healing, including contact with cattle and women.

This separation can be explained as hygiene, and it can also be explained as tradition, and in truth it is both. The wounds are real, and infection is real. But the separation also reinforces the message: you are in a sacred space of transition. You are no longer in ordinary life. You are in a corridor between childhood and adulthood.

When you are fifteen, being placed in that corridor feels like being chosen. It feels like stepping into something serious and respected. Yet, it also feels like you have lost control of your own body for a while. Other people decide what you touch and what you avoid. Other people decide where you sleep. Other people decide what is safe and what is not. And because you are still young, you accept it, even when it feels heavy.

I remember the pain as a constant presence. It was not always sharp, but it was always there. Your forehead becomes the center of your awareness. You become careful with every movement. Even a small

65

facial expression can pull at the healing lines. When you forget and laugh too hard, the skin reminds you. When you turn your head quickly, the skin reminds you. When you sleep and your forehead touches the wrong side of a mat, the skin reminds you.

And with each reminder, the memory of the blood returns.

In my own account, I wrote that I experienced severe blood loss after receiving the marks, and that I appeared lifeless to onlookers and could not respond to their questions. That was not a dramatic description meant to impress. It was a frightening reality. It was the moment when my pride collided with the truth of the body. A boy can promise silence, but he cannot promise how much his blood will flow.

Even after the bleeding stopped, the fear remained. It sat quietly behind me like a shadow. I had not expected my body to react that way. I had not expected to be the boy who looked dead. I had not expected the crowd's energy to change from celebration into alarm.

This is one reason the healing stage is not only about skin. It is also about the mind adjusting to what happened.

The community, of course, does not want to remain in fear. It wants to return to meaning. It wants to see the rite as successful. It wants to see the boy as victorious. That is why the healing process is "eagerly anticipated," and why the community celebrates the completion of the ordeal as the beginning of a new stage of life.

People need that celebration because it turns pain into a story of triumph.

And I needed that story too, at least at first, because the alternative was to sit alone with the reality that I had disobeyed my father for something that nearly overwhelmed me. I did not want to sit with that truth. I wanted to move past it quickly.

Yet the face does not let you move past it quickly.

As my wounds began to close, my scars began to form, and the marks began to look like what they were supposed to look like. That is when the social world started shifting around me.

66

Before scarification, I was still treated as a boy in many conversations, no matter how tall I was, no matter what responsibilities I had already handled in life. But after scarification, people began to treat me differently, and in some ways the difference was immediate. In the wider cultural meaning, the marks are treated as symbols of courage, resilience, and connection to the community, and the ceremony itself reinforces social bonds and celebrates the transition into manhood.

That is the public language.

The private language inside my heart was mixed.

On some days, I felt proud that I had crossed what people called a gate.

On other days, I felt anger at myself for being driven by pressure, and anger at the pressure itself for being so strong that it could defeat my father's counsel. In my earlier writing, I stated clearly that my father refused to consent to the ritual, but I remained fixed in my resolve, driven by the desire to fit in.

That sentence reveals the truth that followed me like a second scar, a scar inside.

My father's warning did not vanish after the ceremony. It became louder.

In fact, it became louder because now every time I touched my forehead, I could hear him. Every time the pain pulsed, I could remember he had tried to stop it. Every time I looked at my reflection, I could remember that these lines were not only culture, they were also stubbornness.

Still, I must be honest about something that may surprise people.

When the scars healed enough for me to see their shape clearly, one of my early private feelings was disappointment. I wrote that I felt secretly disappointed that my scars were not as big as I had dreamed they would be.

That confession is embarrassing in a way, but it is also very human. It shows how the hunger for recognition can survive even after suffering.

I had bled severely, and I had appeared lifeless. Yet part of my mind was still thinking like a teenager who wanted proof, proof that would impress others, proof that would silence anyone who might still see me as small.

That is how deep the desire for belonging can be.

You endure pain, and then you still want the pain to look impressive enough to buy what you wanted.

But time did what pain could not do fully. Time began to mature my thinking.

As I wrote later, I learned that the value of the scars was not in being grand. I came to see their value, if I can call it value, in what the experience represented and the lessons it carried.

This shift did not happen in one week. It happened through life.

Because once the wounds heal, the marks begin their second life.

They begin their life in the eyes of other people.

This is where I learned something that no fifteen-year-old thinks about clearly.

Your face enters a room before your words do.

When you meet someone new, your forehead can tell them a story before you open your mouth. Sometimes that story is accurate in the community that understands the marks. Sometimes it is inaccurate in places where people do not understand them. Sometimes it attracts respect. Sometimes it attracts fear. Sometimes it attracts pity. Sometimes it attracts stereotypes.

The marks are a language, but not everyone reads the language correctly.

Even inside the community, the marks can become a tool of judgment. The community can treat scarification as a marker that separates those who are "men" from those who are still treated as boys. That separation can become harmful when it creates discrimination against those who do not have marks. In the book, I acknowledged that people who opt against the practice can face pressure, alienation, resentment, and tension within their communities.

After I became marked, I began to see this pressure from the other side.

I began to see how easy it is for marked boys to pressure unmarked ones, not necessarily by beating them, but by using words, jokes, and exclusion.

And then a new moral question appeared in my mind, even if I did not frame it like that at first.

If I was pressured, would I become the one who pressures others?

If my dignity felt conditional on scars, would I make another boy feel the same?

If I was afraid of mockery, would I mock others to prove that I now belonged?

That question matters because traditions often survive through repetition, not only of the act, but of the social pressure surrounding it.

The ceremony itself trains boys not only in pain tolerance but also in self-control and composure, because silence is treated as vital during the procedure. That training can build discipline, but it can also build a kind of hardness where boys learn to hide their real feelings. If a boy learns that he must not show pain, he may later think he must not show weakness at all. That can shape how he treats others.

When I moved back into ordinary life after healing, I began to notice the changes.

People began speaking to me with a different weight. People began inviting me into conversations in a different way. My age-mates, the same ones whose pressure had helped push me toward the blade, now treated me as if I had earned something.

And in a sense, I had earned something.

But what I had earned was complicated.

I had earned belonging, but I had also earned permanence.

I had earned a certain social recognition, but I had also earned a visible label I could never hide.

I had earned the right to be treated as a man, but I had also stepped into the expectations that follow manhood, expectations that can be heavy, especially when you are still young inside.

The community expects a marked boy to behave like a man.

And what is "behaving like a man" in a society shaped by cattle camps, conflict, and survival?

Often it means being ready to defend.

Often it means being ready to endure hunger without complaint.

Often it means being ready to face hardship without crying.

Often it means being ready to carry responsibilities early.

Those expectations can build strength, but they can also crush a young person who has not yet developed inner stability.

The scars are supposed to signal readiness, but readiness is not produced instantly by a rite.

A boy can be marked and still be unready.

That is one of the truths I learned slowly.

There is also another truth that grew heavier with time, and it is not only about scars. It is about our land.

In my earlier writing, I noted that several companions who joined me in receiving the marks are no longer alive today, not because of scarification, but because of conflict, vengeance, and animosity in our war-torn homeland.

This is one of the saddest parts of remembering that season.

We stood together, proving bravery to one another, believing we were stepping into manhood.

But the nation itself, and the conflicts within it, had other tests waiting.

War does not care about scars.

Hunger does not care about scars.

Bullets do not pause to read a forehead.

And yet, when boys become men in an environment where violence is common, the rites of passage can sometimes blend into the larger culture of endurance and suffering. It is as if the community trains boys for pain early because pain is expected later.

But if pain is already waiting later, why add more pain earlier?

That question began to disturb me as I matured, especially when I saw the cost of violence on young lives, and when I saw how quickly human beings can be erased.

This is why, even while respecting cultural identity, I began to question the pressure that makes scarification feel compulsory.

Because identity should not be purchased through coercion.

And manhood should not be purchased through blood.

The book also speaks about the wider debates around facial scarification in South Sudan, debates between those who defend it as cultural heritage and those who criticize it because of health and human rights concerns.

At fifteen, I did not think of it as a debate. I thought of it as a requirement.

But as I grew older, and as education and wider exposure expanded the way I think, I began to understand why the debate exists.

Health risks are not theoretical.

When skin is cut, infection is possible.

When tools are shared or not properly sterilized, bloodborne diseases are possible.

The book mentions the risk of transmission of HIV or Hepatitis B, and it acknowledges the pain and infections that can come from the process.

Some people respond by saying we should abandon the practice. Others respond by saying we should preserve it but make it safer. The text itself suggests that modern sterilization methods and disposable instruments can reduce risk, while also admitting that access and affordability can be difficult.

This is a practical conversation. But it is also a deeply emotional one.

Because when you speak of changing the practice, some people feel you are attacking the dignity of the community.

When you speak of maintaining the practice, others feel you are ignoring the health and freedom of the child.

Both sides have pain in their argument.

And I stand in a strange place because my face is part of the evidence.

I am not only speaking as an observer.

I am speaking as someone who was cut.

Someone who bled severely.

Someone whose father warned him.

Someone who was driven by peer pressure.

Someone who later had to live with the decision and the permanence.

That is why, in the book, I wrote that the decision to undergo scarification should be personal and rooted in genuine connection to heritage rather than external pressure, and I warned about the consequences of succumbing to social pressure.

Those lines did not come from reading only.

They came from living.

The scars also began to shape how I thought about pride.

A young boy often confuses pride with dignity. He thinks dignity is something you must prove publicly. He thinks if you do not prove it, you have none. But dignity is not something the crowd gives you. It is something you carry, and it can survive even when you refuse the crowd.

I did not understand that at fifteen.

After the ceremony, as the scars settled into my face, I began to learn that dignity is more about character than about symbols.

This lesson came to me in different ways.

Sometimes it came when I saw men with scars behaving irresponsibly, lying, stealing, or acting cruelly, proving that scars are not character.

Sometimes it came when I saw men without scars behaving with integrity and strength, proving that manhood is not cut into skin.

Sometimes it came when I watched how alcohol can destroy a man faster than any blade. I wrote about acquaintances who seemed to age quickly due to heavy drinking of "aregi," and I contrasted their deterioration with my own preserved youthfulness, which I attributed to God's guidance rather than my own intelligence.

That observation might seem unrelated, but it is not. It belongs to the same theme.

Many young men chase manhood through outward signs, through scars, through drinking, through reckless acts.

But what preserves life is often restraint, discipline, and guidance.

My father's refusal was a form of guidance.

My disobedience was a form of pride.

And my later reflections were shaped by the reality that guidance, not pride, is what keeps a life steady.

The scars also shaped my thinking about how society uses visible symbols to decide who counts.

This is not only about scarification. It is about many things in life.

A uniform can make people respect you, even if your character is weak.

A title can make people listen to you, even if your ideas are empty.

A scar can make people treat you as a man, even if you are still childish inside.

A certificate can make people trust you, even if you do not know how to do the work.

We are human beings, and we are easily fooled by symbols.

Scarification, in our culture, is one of the strongest symbols of all because it is permanent and public.

That is why the face that entered the world first became my teacher.

Each time I met someone new, I could sense the first reading.

In some cases, the reading was respectful.

In other cases, it carried assumptions.

And I began to realize something that made me both sad and alert.

Sometimes, the marks that give you belonging in one environment can make you feel exposed in another.

I began to understand that identity is not always received kindly outside the places that understand it.

That is another part of the cost that young boys do not calculate at fifteen. At fifteen, you calculate only the village, only the cattle camp, only the voices of your peers. You do not calculate the wider world.

But life often pushes you into the wider world.

Education, travel, work, and conflict push people beyond their home circles.

And when you step into places where your scars are not understood, the scars can become something else.

They can become misread.

They can become a reason for others to treat you as strange.

They can become a reason for others to reduce you to stereotypes.

This reality does not automatically mean the practice is wrong, but it does mean the boy should have the right to consider it without being mocked into submission.

This is why the text warns against excessive pressure that forces people into rigid conventions that conflict with their convictions.

That warning is not theory. It is protection.

I have also come to see that community pressure is often defended as "maintaining culture," but in truth, some of that pressure is about control.

When a community makes a practice compulsory, it is not only preserving identity.

It is also controlling bodies.

And when bodies are controlled, individuals become less free to think and choose.

Freedom matters, even inside culture.

Culture without freedom becomes a prison.

This is a hard statement to say in a society where belonging is sacred, but it is still true.

Belonging that requires blood is not the only form of belonging possible.

And if our traditions are truly strong, they should survive without coercion.

The text itself states that traditions are living and change with circumstances, and it suggests alternatives like less invasive forms of body modification, such as tattoos or piercings, as ways to express cultural pride without the same risks.

Some will reject those alternatives and say they are foreign. Some will accept them. I am not writing this chapter to impose alternatives. I am writing it to show that change is not betrayal by default. Sometimes change is survival.

But even if no alternative is adopted, one change must still be made.

Pressure must reduce.

Choice must grow.

A boy should be able to say no without being stripped of dignity.

Because when a boy is pushed into scarification primarily by fear of ridicule, the practice loses its moral meaning.

It becomes fear, not heritage.

It becomes coercion, not identity.

It becomes a social weapon, not a rite of passage.

As I carried the marks into my daily life, I also began to notice how quickly people forget the pain behind symbols.

After healing, people see the finished marks and treat them as normal. They do not see the bleeding. They do not see the pit. They do not see the fear. They see the result and they read it as success.

That is how society works.

It sees results, not processes.

It sees symbols, not wounds.

It sees scars, not blood.

And because it sees only the scar, not the blood, it can demand the scar easily from the next boy, forgetting how much blood might be required.

76

This is one of the reasons I wrote this book.

Because I want the next boy to know what is hidden behind the public symbol.

I want him to know that the story is not only songs and pride.

It is also pain, risk, and regret.

I want him to know that his father's counsel might be stronger than the laughter of his peers.

I want him to know that life is long, and the face is always with you.

And I want him to know that manhood can be built without being cut.

In my earlier writing, I acknowledged something else that matters here. The marks can be seen as a "form of writing," with Dinka and Nuer terms relating scarification to inscription.

If scars are writing, then my life became a reader.

I began reading my own forehead as years passed.

At fifteen, I read it as belonging.

Later, I began reading it as a lesson.

A lesson about how easily a boy can be pushed.

A lesson about how expensive approval can be.

A lesson about how a father's love can be right even when a boy thinks it is blocking him.

A lesson about how fragile life is.

A lesson about how symbols can become idols.

A lesson about how a community can love you and still pressure you in harmful ways.

That is why I call this chapter The Face That Entered the World First.

Because my face entered rooms before my words did.

My face entered conversations before my ideas did.

My face entered life stages before my mind had fully matured into them.

And my face kept reminding me, daily, that some decisions are not undone by regret.

They are only lived through.

This is also where I want to say something that feels important now, as an adult looking back.

I do not regret my people.

I do not regret my identity.

I do not regret the desire to belong.

These things are human and good.

What I regret is the way pressure can twist good desires into harmful decisions.

What I regret is the way a boy can be cornered into permanence when he is still learning how to think for himself.

What I regret is disobeying my father's counsel, not because he wanted to control me, but because he wanted to protect me.

And what I regret is the silence I kept before the ceremony, the silence that allowed fear of ridicule to speak louder than wisdom.

In the next chapter, I will move further into what the marks meant as I grew older, how they followed me into new places and new experiences, and how my understanding of identity, culture, and personal choice continued to change with time.

CHAPTER 8: WHAT THE SCARS COULD NOT DO

When the wounds closed, life resumed its usual rhythm, but it did not resume in the same way. People say, "he healed," as if healing ends the story. Healing only ends the bleeding. It does not end the consequences. It does not end the meanings that the community places on you. It does not end the quiet conversations that happen behind your back. It does not end the new expectations that sit on your shoulders the moment your forehead becomes a public sign.

After scarification, I began to learn what the scars could do.

They could open certain doors of social recognition.

They could change how some elders spoke to me.

They could raise my standing among age-mates who were measuring manhood by visible signs.

They could give me a kind of immediate belonging that I had been desperate to secure.

But as time passed, I also learned what the scars could not do.

They could not protect me from the deeper tests of life.

They could not make me wise overnight.

They could not stop me from feeling fear in situations where fear was normal.

They could not solve the problems of our land.

They could not shield my friends from death.

They could not prevent my mind from questioning what I had done and why I had done it.

The marks were powerful as a symbol, but a symbol does not replace substance. That is a lesson that comes slowly, but when it comes, it changes the way you see everything, not only scarification.

One of the first things I noticed after healing was the social separation.

In our setting, the scarification ceremony is meant to represent a transition into manhood, and it functions as a public confirmation of that transition. The community expects the initiated to carry themselves differently, and the community begins treating them differently. This is one reason the practice has lasted so long. It is not only tradition. It is also a social system of graduation.

At first, I felt relief.

Relief that I was no longer in the uncertain zone, the zone where boys can be questioned and mocked.

Relief that I had done what my age-mates expected.

Relief that I would not have to keep defending my manhood in every small interaction.

But relief is not the same as maturity.

A boy can feel relief and still be unprepared for what comes next.

What comes next is the reality that people now assume you can handle more than you can.

They assume you can carry responsibilities that you have not yet grown into.

They assume you can endure what older men endure.

They assume you can speak as if you have lived longer than you have.

In that sense, the scars can push you into a role you are still learning.

And when you are pushed into a role too quickly, you either grow into it through hardship, or you break quietly inside.

I also noticed something else that surprised me.

The scars did not silence the inner hunger for recognition.

I thought they would.

I thought once I had the marks, the need to prove myself would disappear.

But human desire does not disappear because you satisfy one demand. It often changes shape and returns.

I admitted in my earlier writing that after receiving the scars, I felt secretly disappointed that they were not as big as I had dreamed. This was not a proud confession. It was a confession that revealed how deeply I wanted a visible sign that would impress people.

When I think about that disappointment now, I see it as proof that the problem was not the scars alone.

The problem was the hunger in me, the hunger to be seen, to be respected, to be counted.

The scars could not fix that hunger.

They could only feed it for a moment.

In time, I learned to see the scars differently. I wrote later that I learned to see the value of the scars not in being grand, but in what the experience represented and the lessons it carried.

That shift happened because life kept testing me in ways the scars could not answer.

The first big test the scars could not answer was fear.

Some people imagine that scarification makes a boy fearless. They talk as if enduring that pain means you will never fear anything again. But fear does not work like that. Fear is not removed by one act of endurance. Fear returns when you face real danger, real hunger, real death, and real uncertainty.

And in my life, danger did not wait politely.

I had already lived through threats and conflicts even before the scarification. My childhood was shaped by insecurity, raids, and the sense that life could change suddenly.

Scarification did not stop those realities.

If anything, it placed me more firmly into the category of those expected to face them.

Another test the scars could not answer was moral choice.

The scars do not automatically make you a good man.

They do not stop you from lying.

They do not stop you from being cruel.

They do not stop you from becoming arrogant.

They do not stop you from following a crowd again.

In fact, sometimes the scars can tempt a boy into arrogance, because he begins to think, I have proved myself, therefore I am above correction.

That kind of thinking can ruin a life.

This is why I later wrote that the decision to undergo scarification should be personal and rooted in genuine connection to heritage rather than external pressure, and I warned about the consequences of succumbing to social pressure.

The scars cannot correct the reason you chose them.

If you chose them out of fear of ridicule, then the scars do not remove that fear.

They only hide it behind a symbol.

And hidden fears often return in other forms.

In my case, one of the fears that returned later was the fear of failing expectations.

Once you are scarred, the community assumes you can endure, and that assumption can become another cage.

You are expected to be strong when you are tired.

You are expected to be calm when you are hurting.

You are expected to be silent when you need to speak.

You are expected to be brave when you are frightened.

The ceremony trains silence and composure as signs of self-control and respect. That training can build discipline, but it can also teach a boy to bury emotions instead of handling them in healthy ways.

I began to see this in myself and in others.

Some men are praised for never showing emotion, and they carry that praise into adulthood like a law. They do not cry when they lose a brother. They do not speak when they are overwhelmed. They drink instead. They fight instead. They harden instead.

That is not strength.

That is a slow collapse disguised as strength.

The scars cannot teach emotional wisdom. Only life and good guidance can.

Then there was the test of health.

The scars do not come without risk.

Even after healing, the story of risk remains. The process can inflict pain, cause infections, and carry the risk of transmission of HIV or Hepatitis B.

Some people say, "But it has been done for generations, so it is safe."

Generations doing something does not automatically make it safe. It only means people survived it enough to keep doing it. Many died silently, or suffered complications, and their stories are not always recorded.

In my own case, I experienced severe blood loss and appeared lifeless. That alone is enough to say the practice is not harmless.

I did survive, and I am grateful.

But survival does not turn risk into safety.

One of the deepest tests the scars could not answer was the test of loss.

The scars did not protect my companions.

I wrote that several companions who joined me in receiving the marks are no longer alive today, not because of scarification, but because of conflict, vengeance, and animosity in our war-torn homeland.

That line has stayed in my heart like a second scar.

It reminds me that life's biggest threats in our land are often not cultural rites, but violence and instability.

But it also raises another question.

If our homeland already produces enough suffering through war and revenge, why add extra suffering to our children through coercive rites?

That question became harder for me to ignore as I grew older.

The scars could not protect anyone from a bullet.

They could not stop an ambush.

They could not stop hunger.

They could not stop the collapse of a community into cycles of revenge.

In that sense, the scars are small compared to the larger storms, yet they are also part of the same culture of endurance and pain.

The difference is this.

Some pain is unavoidable, because life is harsh.

Other pain is chosen, and the choice is often driven by pressure.

The scars are in the second category, especially when boys are coerced.

That is why the moral weight of scarification becomes serious. When pain is forced, it becomes injustice.

As I carried the scars forward, I began to see another truth.

The scars could not give me a good name in the deeper sense.

I had wanted a good name from a young age. I admitted that I longed to earn respected standing among my people, and that this desire was one of the driving forces behind my decision.

But a good name is not a pattern on the forehead.

A good name is behavior.

It is integrity.

It is how you treat people when nobody is watching.

It is how you handle power when you have it.

It is whether you keep your word.

It is whether you protect the weak.

It is whether you humble yourself when you are wrong.

The scars cannot do that for you.

They can only give you a first impression.

And first impressions can be false.

I have seen men with scars who are irresponsible.

I have seen men without scars who are wise and disciplined.

That comparison taught me what the scars could not do.

They could not manufacture character.

Character is built in other ways.

Another thing the scars could not do was solve the question of identity.

This may sound strange, because scars are often defended as identity.

But identity is not only what you carry on your skin. Identity is also what you believe, what you value, and how you live.

A person can be scarred and still feel lost inside.

A person can be unscarred and still know who he is.

A person can carry cultural marks and still betray his culture through his actions.

This is why identity cannot be reduced to one rite.

The text acknowledges that traditions are living entities that change with circumstances and needs. If traditions change, then identity must be able to survive change. If identity collapses because a method changes, then the identity was too fragile.

This is why I began to think differently about heritage.

Heritage is not only scarification.

Heritage is language.

Heritage is values.

Heritage is the way we honor elders.

Heritage is the way we raise children.

Heritage is the way we treat guests.

Heritage is the way we handle conflict.

Heritage is the way we seek peace.

If scarification disappears tomorrow, these other things can remain, and they must remain if we want to stay ourselves.

This is why the debate about scarification needs careful thought, not only emotional defense.

The text describes long debates in South Sudan between those who defend scarification as cultural heritage and those who condemn it for health and human rights concerns. In those debates, people often speak as if abandoning scarification means abandoning the tribe itself.

But the deeper question is this.

Can we keep the meaning and reduce the harm?

Can we keep the dignity and remove coercion?

Can we keep belonging and remove ridicule?

Can we keep identity and protect health?

Those questions matter because no tradition is worth the death or trauma of children.

Even those who strongly defend scarification do not want boys to die.

They want boys to carry identity.

So if the goal is identity, then methods should be questioned when methods create avoidable danger.

The text suggests that modern sterilization methods and disposable instruments can reduce risk, while acknowledging that access and affordability can be challenging. It also suggests exploring alternatives such as tattoos or piercings, as less invasive forms of expressing cultural pride.

Whether or not one agrees with those suggestions, one truth remains.

The scars could not make the decision moral if the decision was coerced.

That is why pressure must be confronted.

Pressure is the hidden blade.

Pressure is the part nobody wants to admit, because admitting it would mean admitting that the rite is not purely voluntary.

In my case, peer pressure drove me, and my father refused consent, yet I still went through with it because I wanted to fit in.

When I say that now, I am not saying it to shame myself only.

I am saying it because many boys are driven by the same force, and they deserve honesty from those of us who already carry the marks.

They deserve elders who can say, "We will not mock you if you refuse."

They deserve age-mates who can say, "We will still respect you."

They deserve families who can stand for them, even if the crowd is loud.

Because the scars cannot protect you from regret.

Regret has its own sharpness.

It may not be visible like a scar, but it can cut you internally for years.

In my own story, I carried regret not only about the marks, but about disobeying my father. He had warned me, and I ignored him. That regret matured into respect, and that respect matured into a broader understanding of what wisdom looks like.

Wisdom is not loud.

Wisdom does not always win the crowd.

Wisdom often speaks softly and waits for you to realize, later, that it was right.

That is another thing the scars could not do.

They could not make me wise.

But they did contribute to the lessons that made me wiser later.

Not because scars are wisdom, but because scars can become reminders, and reminders can force a person to think.

This is why I am careful when I speak about them now.

I am not trying to tell every community to abandon their ways.

I am not trying to insult my people.

I am trying to tell the truth about what it costs and what it cannot give.

The scars can give you social recognition.

They can give you belonging.

They can connect you to heritage.

But they cannot replace character.

They cannot guarantee safety.

They cannot prevent loss.

They cannot stop violence.

They cannot manufacture maturity.

And they cannot erase the fact that a boy deserves choice.

So, if the scars could not do these things, what could?

The answer is not a ceremony.

The answer is raising.

The answer is teaching.

The answer is elders who guide boys into responsibility through daily discipline, not only through one rite.

The answer is communities that praise integrity more than endurance of pain.

The answer is families that protect boys from ridicule.

The answer is fathers whose counsel is honored, not laughed at.

This is where my father returns again in the story, not because I am trying to idealize him, but because he represents something we often ignore.

He refused to consent.

That refusal was not weakness.

It was protection.

It was a different kind of courage, the courage to stand against the crowd for the sake of a child.

That is the kind of courage we need more of if we want to preserve life without destroying dignity.

As I continued growing, the scars remained on my forehead, but my mind continued changing.

In the next chapter, I will move into the deeper reflections that came with age, the way my understanding of culture and personal choice matured, and how my scars began to function not as a trophy, but as a lifelong question.

CHAPTER 9: THE FACE I CARRY, THE LIFE I CHOOSE

The mirror does not argue.

There is a kind of silence a mirror gives you. It does not praise you. It does not insult you. It simply shows you what is there, and then leaves you alone with your thoughts.

For many years, my forehead has spoken before my mouth. Even when I say nothing, the lines say something. They tell a story of a boy who wanted to be seen, a boy who wanted a good name, a boy who feared being left behind by his age-mates, a boy who did not yet understand that some choices do not grow old with you. They grow with you.

When I was younger, I used to look at my scars and measure them like a child measures everything. Are they big enough? Are they clear enough? Will people notice them? I carried that strange hunger that young boys often carry, the hunger to be counted among men, to be recognized, to be called brave, to stand inside the circle and not outside it.

Later, my eyes changed. The mirror stayed the same, but my eyes changed. I began to measure something else. Not the size of the scars, but the weight of the story behind them. Not how visible they were, but what they had already cost me, and what they could still cost me in a world that is no longer arranged the way our villages were arranged.

I also began to measure what they gave me, because life is not only one-sided. It is never only shame, and never only pride. It is usually both, fighting inside the same skin.

Sometimes I touch my forehead without thinking. It is like touching a chapter in a book you wrote with blood, without pen. And every time my fingers pass over those lines, I remember the first person who tried to stop me.

My father, Maluth Abiel Kueth, did not want me to receive those marks. He advised me against it, with the seriousness of a father who can already see the road ahead, even when his son only sees today.

In my younger mind, his advice felt like a delay, like a refusal to let me reach manhood. In my older mind, his advice feels like love in its strictest form. Love that does not clap for your excitement. Love that tries to save you from your own heat.

I did not listen. And because I did not listen, I have had to listen in another way, through experience, through consequences, through long nights of thinking, through the slow education that pain gives.

This chapter is not written to condemn a whole people. It is not written to mock our cultures. It is also not written to pretend that culture is untouchable. I have learned that culture can be wise and still be questioned. Culture can be beautiful and still be harmful. Culture can build a person and still break another.

So I will speak as one who belongs, and as one who has suffered inside belonging.

Section: The scars follow you beyond the cattle camp

In the village, scarification has its own language. It is read the way a passport is read in an airport. It tells people who you are, where you belong, what age-group you stand with, what you have endured, and what you can be trusted to endure again.

In the village, many things are forgiven because they are understood. Even mistakes can be absorbed by the community because the community knows you, knows your father, knows your mother, knows your clan, knows your childhood. A boy can make a foolish choice and still be carried by the warm hands of familiar people.

But the world outside does not know your childhood. It does not know your clan. It does not know the rules that shaped you. It only sees your face, and then it forms its own story. And sometimes that story is cruel.

I have walked into spaces where my forehead entered before I did. I have seen curiosity. I have seen suspicion. I have seen laughter hiding behind politeness. I have seen people stare and then quickly look away as if they were caught doing something wrong.

I have also met people who asked with respect, and people who listened like students, not like judges. Those moments are rare, but they are healing. They remind me that human beings are capable of learning if you speak to them with patience.

Still, I cannot lie. The scars have complicated my life in ways I did not predict when I was fifteen.

When you are a boy chasing approval, you think your whole life will remain in the village. You think the rules of the cattle camp will follow you everywhere. You do not imagine visas. You do not imagine interviews. You do not imagine offices. You do not imagine school systems that teach the world as if your world never existed.

And even when you do imagine travel, you imagine it like a dream. You do not imagine the daily small humiliations that can come with being marked in a place that does not honor the meaning of the marks.

There is also another reality. Sometimes, the scars are not the problem. Sometimes the problem is the way we talk about them, the way we defend them, the way we fight over them like a political party fights over a flag. Sometimes the scars become a weapon in the mouth, not a symbol on the skin.

I have seen young men use scarification as proof that they are superior to others. I have seen them use it to insult those who did not receive the marks. I have seen them act as if pain itself makes a person moral, as if endurance makes a person wise.

But I have also seen young men without scars become more disciplined, more educated, more responsible, more faithful, more kind, more useful to their communities than many scarred men who never outgrew their pride.

So what is the true measure of a man? Is it the cut on the forehead, or the cut he makes in the world through his character and service?

That question has stayed with me for years. And it has forced me to re-check my own heart.

Section: What I thought bravery was, and what it became

When I was young, I thought bravery was silence in pain. I thought bravery was not crying. I thought bravery was not shaking. I thought bravery was not begging. I thought bravery was walking into what frightens you and coming out with a visible proof that you did not run.

That is why scarification appeals to young boys. It gives them a stage. It gives them a test. It gives them a badge. It gives them a story they can repeat, and a story others can see without hearing it.

I even remember a strange disappointment I carried, quietly, after my scars healed. I expected them to be bigger. I expected them to look like the scars of those older boys whose foreheads looked like maps carved by fire. My own scars were not as loud as I expected, and my young pride felt cheated.

But over time, I learned something that changed me. The value of my scars was never in how big they were. The value was in what they taught me about pressure, about choices, about regret, and about the danger of copying others when you have not asked yourself who you are.

That lesson is heavier than any scar.

I also learned that bravery is not only about enduring pain. Bravery is also about enduring misunderstanding. Bravery is also about saying, "I was wrong," even when your friends want you to pretend you were right. Bravery is also about choosing a new path when your community expects you to keep walking the old one.

Bravery is about character. It is about discipline. It is about responsibility. It is about being honest with yourself.

Sometimes, bravery is refusing the blade.

In the years since my scarification, I have met many boys who stand where I once stood. They are surrounded by voices. Their friends call them cowards if they hesitate. Their elders call them boys if they delay. Their hearts want belonging. Their eyes want approval.

And I want to tell them what I could not tell myself then.

Belonging that requires you to destroy part of your future is not belonging. It is a trap wearing the clothes of tradition.

Section: The father I tried to outrun

There is a special pain in remembering a father's warning after you have already stepped into the thing he warned you about.

My father's counsel against my forehead marks was not a casual suggestion. It was serious. It came from love, and from wisdom that was older than my excitement.

When I chose scarification, I was not only choosing a ritual. I was also choosing to ignore a voice that was trying to protect me. And because fathers carry a deep place in the soul of a son, the guilt of ignoring a father does not die quickly.

That is why I later dedicated this story to him. The dedication is not decoration. It is confession. It is also gratitude.

As I grew older, I began to see how a father thinks.

A father thinks in years, not in days.

A father thinks about what will happen when the boy leaves the village.

A father thinks about the kind of world that is coming, even when the boy thinks the world will never change.

And when I look at my life now, I cannot deny it. My father's concern had reasons.

Even in our own communities, practices change. Age-sets shift. Names remain, but meanings stretch. Some groups did not practice scarification in earlier age-sets, and later they adopted it. Some age-sets carried no scarification, then later ones did.

That alone should humble us. It should remind us that "this is how we have always done it" is sometimes a lie, or at least an incomplete story.

Our communities are living. They grow. They borrow. They adapt. They stop some things. They begin other things.

So if culture can change, then it can also be guided.

My father was guiding me, but I did not accept the guidance then. Now I accept it, late, with scars on my forehead.

Section: The debate that refuses to die

One of the strangest things about scarification is that it is both personal and political.

It is personal because it is on a person's skin. It is pain in flesh. It is memory in the body.

It is political because people use it to define identity, to draw boundaries, to mark who is inside and who is outside.

Even the question of who started facial scarification becomes a debate filled with heat. Some people argue it came through colonial systems, used as a tool to separate groups. Others argue it existed long before, and that it is deeply rooted in African ways of life.

I have listened to elders. I have listened to peers. I have listened to those who love the practice and those who hate it.

And I have learned something simple.

Sometimes, people do not argue because they want truth. They argue because they want to win.

But cultural questions are not sports. They are life. And life is not helped by shouting.

The truth may not be simple. It may even be mixed.

A practice can be indigenous and still be shaped by colonial rule later.

A practice can have spiritual meaning and still be used as a tool of control.

A practice can be loved by many and still be regretted by some.

I remember one statement that stayed with me from an interview in the book, a man saying he wished he could remove his scars, even though they were not as visible as others.

That one voice matters. It breaks the lie that everyone loves scarification. It forces us to admit that inside any culture there are different hearts, different experiences, different regrets.

And if scarification is forced, or carried mainly by pressure, then it stops being a proud identity and becomes a wound of conformity.

Section: Names, language, and the deeper markings

As I grew older, I began to care about language. Not only English, but our own languages too. Because I learned that sometimes the deepest marks in a community are not on the forehead. They are in the words people use.

Words can build a person. Words can also reduce a person.

In some communities, terms for "man" carry meanings that also touch "husband," "father," "human being." These meanings can be mistranslated and misunderstood, and that misunderstanding can create insult where there was none.

When I began to notice how often outsiders misunderstand our words and our practices, I also began to notice how often we misunderstand ourselves.

Sometimes we defend scarification as if it is the only proof of being a man. That is misunderstanding.

Sometimes we mock those without scars as if they are less human. That is misunderstanding.

Sometimes we talk about our own people with cheap stereotypes because we have absorbed the language of people who looked down on us. That is misunderstanding too.

Language is a kind of scarification. It marks the mind. It shapes identity. It defines what you respect and what you despise.

And if our words are careless, our communities become careless.

This is why I believe that education is not the enemy of culture. Education can be the tool that cleans culture from lies, from misuse, from cruelty, from forced practices disguised as tradition.

Education can also help us speak about scarification without insulting ourselves and without insulting others.

Section: Generations change, and the world does not ask permission

When I look at younger boys today, I see that their world is not the world I grew up in.

They have phones. They have the internet. They have cities. They have new dreams. They have exposure to ideas that would have sounded strange to my younger ears.

They also have new pressures.

In the past, pressure came mostly from your village and your peers.

Now pressure comes from everywhere.

It comes from movies. It comes from social media. It comes from global fashion. It comes from politics. It comes from religious arguments. It comes from shame and praise delivered in seconds.

So I understand why some young people reject scarification. They are trying to survive in a world that judges them by global standards.

I also understand why some young people defend scarification with anger. They feel their identity is under attack, and anger becomes a shield.

But anger is not a plan.

The question is not, "Should we become like the West?"

The question is not, "Should we keep everything from the past?"

The question is: "How do we live with dignity in both worlds without losing ourselves?"

For me, the answer begins with choice.

A culture that forces permanent markings without real consent is a culture that needs correction.

A culture that teaches boys to insult others over scars is a culture that needs correction.

A culture that cannot face medical risks honestly is a culture that needs correction.

At the same time, a modern world that laughs at African identity is also sick.

A modern world that calls every African practice primitive without learning its meaning is also sick.

So we must be careful. We must not throw away ourselves while trying to fix ourselves.

We must not become enemies of our own people just because we learned English.

We must not become slaves of global opinions just because we travel.

Section: What I would tell the boy I was

If I could sit with my fifteen-year-old self, I would not start with insults.

I would start with understanding. Because the boy I was wanted something real.

He wanted respect.

He wanted belonging.

He wanted a good name.

He feared being treated like a child.

He feared being laughed at.

He feared being left behind.

Those fears are human. And if we do not understand the fears, we will never help the boys who carry them today.

But after understanding, I would tell him this:

Your worth is not in a cut.

Your manhood is not in the blade.

Your future is longer than this season.

The friends who push you today will not carry your consequences tomorrow.

The community that praises you today might not protect you later when the world judges you differently.

I would also tell him to listen to his father.

Because a father's warning is sometimes a bridge God places in your path.

And I would tell him that real bravery includes the bravery to wait.

Wait until you understand.

Wait until you can decide freely, not under threats of mockery.

Wait until you can explain your decision to yourself without using the word "everyone."

When a boy says, "Everyone is doing it," he is admitting that he is not choosing. He is being chosen by pressure.

Section: The lesson I now offer to others

In the earlier part of this work, I acknowledged openly that this is a personal story and not a fully researched account. But even when a story is personal, it can still carry a message that helps others avoid a trap.

That is why I want to speak clearly to parents, elders, and young people.

To parents: talk to your children early. Do not wait until the peer group has already trained them. Explain the meaning of practices, yes, but also explain the risks. If you believe in scarification, do not force it. If you oppose it, do not insult your own culture while opposing it. Teach with respect, not with shame.

To elders: remember that culture is not a prison. Culture is a home. A home should not crush its children. A home should raise them. If a practice is harming young people, you do not lose your identity by adjusting it. You show wisdom by guiding it. Even age-set practices have shifted over time. So do not pretend that change is betrayal. Sometimes change is protection.

To young people: do not let pain become your only measure of value. Do not believe that scars automatically make you disciplined. Do not confuse crowd approval with inner peace. If you choose scarification, let it be your choice, not your fear. If you reject it, reject it with respect, not with hatred for your own people.

And to all of us: let us stop using scarification as a reason to divide. We already have too many ways to divide. A nation cannot be built by mocking parts of itself.

Section: The scars do not end the story

Sometimes people look at facial marks and assume the person is trapped in the past.

They do not know that a person can be marked and still think forward.

They do not know that a person can regret and still grow.

They do not know that a person can carry a scar and still build a life that is larger than the scar.

I have learned to hold my story with both hands.

One hand holds the cultural meaning, the belonging, the memories of the village, the faces of elders, the sound of people celebrating a boy becoming a man.

The other hand holds the regret, the lessons, the complicated experiences outside the village, the misunderstandings, the times I wished I could hide my forehead, the moments I felt my father's warning like a weight.

Both hands are true.

And because both hands are true, I do not want to lie to anyone reading this.

If you are reading this with scars on your forehead, I am not your enemy. I know what it is to carry visible identity.

If you are reading this without scars, I am not here to call you less. I have seen scarless men act with more honor than many scarred men.

If you are reading this as an outsider, I am not asking you to praise our practices blindly. I am asking you to learn before you judge.

And if you are reading this as a young boy standing near that decision, I am asking you to be careful with your life.

Because your body is a book. And once you write certain lines, they will travel with you into places you have not yet imagined.

For me, these lines on my forehead have become a lifelong teacher.

They taught me about pressure.

They taught me about identity.

They taught me about fatherhood and wisdom.

They taught me about the difference between what a community praises and what a life requires.

And maybe, if I tell the story with honesty, they can teach someone else too.

Not by forcing them to copy my mistake, but by helping them avoid it.

That, for me, is one way the scars can stop being only scars and become a warning sign, a guidepost, a lesson.

A face can be marked, but a life can still be chosen.

PART III
CHAPTER 10: THE SCARS OF A BOY, THE SCARS OF A NATION

When a private wound meets a public wound.

There is a point in life when you realize your personal story is not separate from the story of your people. You may want it to be separate. You may try to keep it private, like a small secret between you and your mirror. But the truth is that we carry each other. A boy carries the community in his habits and fears, and the community carries the boy in its expectations and rules.

That is why I could never fully treat my scarification as only my business.

Yes, the blade touched my skin, not the skin of my neighbors.

Yes, the blood that filled that pit was mine, not theirs.

Yes, the weakness that made me appear lifeless was mine, not theirs.

But the pressure that drove me was not mine alone. It was social. The desire to fit in was not created by my blood. It was created by the hunger for belonging that communities plant in boys very early.

And the meaning that people read on my forehead was not created by me either. It was created by tradition, by expectation, by the long habit of treating marks as proof of passage.

So the moment I healed and stepped back into ordinary life, I was no longer only dealing with what happened to me.

I was also dealing with the story that the community wanted to tell through me.

They wanted to say, this boy has become a man.

They wanted to say, our ways still stand.

They wanted to say, our age-group has crossed.

They wanted to say, our identity continues.

Those statements are powerful. They can build pride, unity, and continuity.

But they can also hide a dangerous truth, the truth that culture can sometimes pressure children into permanent decisions before they are ready to judge what permanence means.

As I grew older, another thought began to sit in my mind like a stone.

If we can pressure a boy into cutting his face, what else can we pressure him into?

If a community can mock a boy until he surrenders his forehead, what else can that same community mock him into doing?

If the crowd can defeat a father's warning, what else can the crowd defeat?

This is where my scarification began to feel like a small example of a larger problem.

And that larger problem is not only cultural. It is national.

Section: The habit of coercion

One of the hardest things to admit about ourselves, as communities and as a nation, is that we have a habit of coercion.

We do not always call it coercion. We call it discipline. We call it tradition. We call it loyalty. We call it unity. We call it respect.

But in practice, it often looks like this.

Agree, or you will be mocked.

Join us, or you will be excluded.

Support this, or you are a traitor.

Carry this mark, or you are not one of us.

Say the right words, or you will be punished.

Coercion can be loud, and it can be quiet. Sometimes it uses violence. Sometimes it uses shame.

In my case, shame was the weapon.

Peer pressure was the force.

And my father's refusal was the small voice that almost saved me, but did not, because I wanted approval more than protection.

When I look at our national life, I see the same pattern in bigger clothing.

Many of our conflicts begin the same way my scarification began.

A group demands conformity.

A person hesitates.

The crowd applies pressure.

The hesitant person is called weak, called disloyal, called something worse.

Then fear takes over.

Then a person chooses survival or belonging in the group instead of listening to wisdom or conscience.

In a cattle camp, this can end with scars.

In a nation, it can end with graves.

This is why I say my forehead is not only about a personal rite.

It is also a warning about the danger of social pressure when it becomes a substitute for reason and consent.

Section: My father's refusal and the kind of leadership we lack

There is a kind of leadership that does not exist much in our public life, and I learned it first through my father's refusal.

My father did not consent to my scarification. He advised me not to do it.

Whether people agree with his position or not, his stance reveals a form of courage that is rare.

It is the courage to stand against a crowd for the sake of a child.

It is the courage to protect a life even when the community says protection is weakness.

It is the courage to be misunderstood today so that your child might thank you tomorrow.

That is leadership.

Not the leadership of shouting slogans.

Not the leadership of collecting praise.

Not the leadership of forcing others to clap.

Leadership that protects.

Leadership that restrains harm.

Leadership that says no when yes is popular.

Now compare that to how we often operate at national level.

We reward leaders who make noise.

We reward leaders who threaten.

We reward leaders who mobilize fear.

We reward leaders who can force compliance.

We do not reward leaders who protect children from harmful pressure.

We do not reward leaders who choose restraint.

We do not reward leaders who speak softly and still stand firmly.

If we had more leaders with the spirit of my father's refusal, our politics would be less violent, our youth would be less disposable, and our communities would be more humane.

That is not a romantic statement. It is practical.

Because a nation is not built only by roads and buildings. A nation is built by the moral habits of its people.

And if the moral habit is coercion, then the nation will always be unstable.

Section: The scars that became proof, and the proof that became a burden

When a society treats a visible sign as proof, it changes how people behave.

Scarification becomes proof of courage.

But then courage becomes a performance.

Silence under pain becomes a badge.

But then silence becomes a habit even when speaking would save lives.

Enduring becomes a requirement.

But then people endure injustice without challenging it, because they were trained to endure, not trained to question.

Our scarification rite trains composure and silence as markers of self-control and respect.

This training has benefits, but it also carries a risk, especially in a society already wounded by violence.

Because sometimes the most dangerous thing is not a lack of endurance.

Sometimes the most dangerous thing is too much endurance.

A people can endure abuse until abuse becomes normal.

A people can endure corruption until corruption becomes culture.

A people can endure division until division becomes identity.

So the question becomes, what should we teach our boys to endure, and what should we teach them to reject?

If we train boys only to be silent under the knife, we may produce men who are silent under injustice.

If we teach boys that a good name comes from pain, we may produce men who chase pain and produce pain.

This is why I have come to believe that a rite alone cannot be the heart of our definition of manhood.

Manhood must be redefined around responsibility, integrity, and service, not only around endurance of pain.

Section: The part of the story people do not like to hear

There is a part of my story that some people do not like to hear because it makes the rite look less heroic.

I bled severely.

I appeared lifeless.

I could not respond to people's questions.

Many prefer to hear only the proud version, the version where the boy is strong and silent and then stands up smiling like a warrior.

My version includes fear.

It includes weakness.

It includes the truth that the body can betray your pride.

This truth matters because many young boys are pressured using stories that hide the risk.

They are told, you will be fine.

They are told, you must not fear.

They are told, your ancestors did it.

They are told, you will become a man.

But nobody tells them, you might lose a frightening amount of blood.

Nobody tells them, you might faint and look dead.

Nobody tells them, you might carry regret for ignoring your father's warning.

Nobody tells them, your scars will follow you into places where people will misread them.

So I insist on telling the less comfortable version because I do not want boys to be recruited into permanent decisions using only half-truths.

Section: Traditions change, so why do we pretend they cannot?

One of the strongest arguments used to defend scarification is the claim that it has always been done, and therefore it must continue.

But even inside our own histories, practices have shifted.

Some age-sets did not practice scarification, while later age-sets adopted it.

That fact alone should calm the debates.

It means that culture has moved before.

It means that change is not automatically betrayal.

It means that people have already adjusted their practices in response to new realities.

And our realities have changed drastically.

We have cities now.

We have schools.

We have hospitals.

We have different patterns of employment.

We have new diseases.

We have new travel.

We have new legal systems.

We have global communication.

We have youth who live in multiple worlds at the same time.

So it is not strange to ask whether practices should be adjusted.

What is strange is to treat questions as insults.

A tradition that cannot be questioned becomes a dictator.

A tradition that cannot be questioned becomes an idol.

And idols always demand blood.

Section: The debate about origins and the deeper question of meaning

There are also debates about where scarification came from and why it spread in certain ways. Some people argue that scarification in South Sudan became widespread through colonial systems, used as a way to separate groups. Others argue that it existed long before and should not be blamed on outsiders.

I have listened to these debates, and I have learned that arguing about origins can sometimes distract from the deeper question.

Even if a practice is ancient, the question remains.

Does it still serve life today?

Even if a practice is indigenous, the question remains.

Does it still protect the child, or does it mainly protect the pride of the group?

Even if a practice is meaningful, the question remains.

Can the meaning be kept without coercion and without unnecessary risk?

Because culture should serve humans, not the other way around.

Humans are not made for culture.

Culture is made for humans.

So when a culture begins to harm humans, especially children, it must be corrected by the same wisdom that created it.

Section: The voices that break the myth of universal love

Another reason I cannot speak about scarification as if it is universally embraced is that even among scarred men, there are those who regret it.

In the book, there is a voice of a man who wished he could remove his scars, even though they were not as visible as others.

That voice matters.

It tells us that not everyone experiences scarification as pride.

It tells us that some carry it as a burden.

It tells us that some would reverse it if reversal were possible.

If such men exist, then the moral responsibility of the community increases.

Because it means that coercion can create lifelong regret, not just a short season of pain.

It also means we should stop treating every critique of scarification as an attack on identity.

Sometimes critique is simply pain trying to speak.

Sometimes critique is regret trying to be heard.

Sometimes critique is a wounded person asking the community to become gentler.

Section: The scars of my companions and the cruelty of our larger wars

When I remember the day of my scarification, I do not see only my face. I also see the faces of those who stood near me. The companions who went through the rite around the same time.

And then, when I move forward in time, I remember that some of those companions are no longer alive.

Not because scarification killed them, but because our homeland has been torn by conflict, vengeance, and animosity.

This is where the chapter becomes heavier.

Because it forces me to ask, what did our rites prepare us for, and what did they fail to prepare us for?

They prepared us to endure pain.

They prepared us to be silent.

They prepared us to be tough.

But did they prepare us to resist cycles of revenge?

Did they prepare us to build institutions?

Did they prepare us to protect civilians?

Did they prepare us to forgive?

Did they prepare us to choose peace over pride?

A nation is not saved by toughness alone.

A nation is saved by moral discipline, by truth, by fairness, and by the ability to see the other as human even when you disagree.

If we can cut a child's face in the name of identity, but cannot stop cutting each other in the name of politics and tribe, then something is deeply broken in our priorities.

This is why I call this chapter The Scars of a Boy, the Scars of a Nation.

Because our land is covered in wounds, not on the forehead, but in graves and camps and burned homes and broken families.

And those wounds are far more urgent than any rite.

Yet, rites can teach us something about how we create wounds.

They show us that we can normalize harm when harm is wrapped in tradition and praise.

War does the same thing.

War normalizes harm.

War wraps harm in slogans.

War demands conformity.

War punishes those who hesitate.

War turns young men into tools.

So when I speak against coercion in scarification, I am also speaking against coercion in politics and in conflict.

Because the same spirit is involved.

Section: If I could choose again, what would I keep and what would I change?

I cannot choose again. That is the nature of scars.

But I can choose how I interpret them.

I can choose what message to take from them.

I can choose what message to offer to others.

If I could keep one thing from the rite, it would be the sense of community responsibility, the idea that a boy is not raised alone, that the community is involved in shaping him.

That communal care is valuable.

Our modern life is too individualistic in many ways. People disappear into their private lives and forget the strength of shared responsibility.

If I could change one thing, it would be the method of enforcing identity through shame.

I would remove ridicule.

I would remove coercion.

I would remove the idea that a boy without scars is less.

Because the moment you remove coercion, you allow culture to breathe.

And you allow boys to become men through conviction, not through fear.

If we must mark identity, let it be through education in language, history, and values.

Let it be through service.

Let it be through responsibility.

Let it be through rites that do not demand permanent injury as the price of belonging.

The book itself treats traditions as living and suggests that practices can be adjusted, including through safer methods or alternatives, recognizing the changing circumstances of modern life.

Whether one accepts those alternatives or not, the principle is clear.

Change is possible.

Choice is necessary.

Section: The life I choose now

One statement I made earlier in my writing is that this is a personal story, not a fully researched work.

That matters because my aim is not to win an academic debate. My aim is to tell what happened, what it cost, and what it taught me.

What it taught me is this.

A person can inherit a culture and still think.

A person can love his people and still correct what harms children.

A person can carry scars and still advocate for choice.

A person can belong and still refuse coercion.

A person can admit regret without hating his identity.

So the life I choose now is not to fight my people.

It is to speak truth inside belonging.

It is to honor my father's wisdom, even late.

It is to warn boys about the power of peer pressure.

It is to remind elders that traditions have shifted before, and they can shift again without collapsing identity.

It is to remind all of us that culture must not be used as an excuse to harm children.

And it is to connect this personal lesson to a national lesson.

If we want South Sudan to heal, we must reduce the habit of coercion everywhere.

In families.

In cattle camps.

In schools.

In politics.

In armies.

In churches.

In tribes.

We must replace coercion with consent.

We must replace ridicule with guidance.

We must replace pride with responsibility.

We must replace fear with truth.

Because a nation cannot become peaceful if it keeps training its children to surrender to pressure.

Section: Closing of the chapter

When I touch my forehead now, I do not touch it as a trophy.

I touch it as a reminder.

A reminder of what I endured.

A reminder of how close weakness can come to a proud boy.

A reminder of my father's love that tried to protect me.

A reminder that not all tradition is automatically good, and not all change is automatically betrayal.

A reminder that our nation's larger wounds demand more serious courage than any blade can test.

And a reminder that the greatest mark a man can carry is not on his forehead.

It is in his character.

It is in his restraint.

It is in his willingness to choose life over pride.

It is in his willingness to protect children, even from the crowd.

That is the kind of man I am still trying to become.

CHAPTER 11: A LETTER WRITTEN FOR TOMORROW

I did not write this for applause.

There is a kind of writing that is done to impress people, and there is a kind of writing that is done to free the heart. When I began putting this story into words, I did not feel like a hero. I felt like a man trying to tell the truth about a choice I could not undo.

That is why I have kept returning to the same core realities.

My father warned me, and I did not listen.

Peer pressure drove me, and I surrendered my forehead to a decision that was bigger than my age.

The day of the ritual was not only about bravery. It was also about danger. I bled severely and appeared lifeless, unable to respond to people's questions.

I have repeated these points not because I enjoy repeating pain, but because these are the facts that most people prefer to keep hidden behind the public pride of the practice.

Some people want the story of scars to remain simple.

They want it to be only pride.

They want it to be only tradition.

They want it to be only courage.

But I have come to understand that a simple story can become a trap, especially for the next boy who is still easy to manipulate, still hungry for approval, still too young to measure the weight of permanence.

So this chapter is for tomorrow.

It is for the people who will come after me and ask, why did you do it, and what did it mean, and what would you advise us to do with our own lives?

Section: The question nobody wants to answer clearly

As I grew older, I began hearing the same question in many forms, in villages and in towns, in quiet conversations and in loud arguments.

Should we abandon our traditions and hide our cultural practices to avoid discrimination and mistreatment?

Or should we stand firm and fight for recognition and validation of these practices?

The book itself states that there is no easy answer, and that the real challenge is balancing pride in heritage with the pursuit of dignity and respect in all areas of life.

That statement is honest.

It tells the truth that both sides carry something valid.

One side fears loss of identity. They look at the modern world and see disrespect for African ways, and they do not want their children to grow up ashamed of their own people.

The other side fears harm. They look at the medical risks, the forced pressure, the lifelong regret that some carry, and they do not want their children to be injured in the name of belonging.

If you are wise, you do not mock either side.

If you are wise, you admit that both sides are trying to protect something.

But the hard part is choosing what protection looks like in real life, not in slogans.

For me, the answer begins where it always began, with one child, one face, one father, one choice.

Because culture is not an abstract argument. Culture is lived on the skin of real people.

And scarification, especially facial scarification, is not reversible.

That means the moral weight is heavier than most people admit.

If it were something temporary, like a ceremony that leaves no permanent mark, the argument would be lighter.

But when the mark becomes a lifetime companion, the child deserves a deeper level of protection than ridicule and pressure.

Section: The older I became, the more I saw the pressure clearly

When I was fifteen, I did not describe it as pressure. I described it as life. I described it as normal. I described it as what everyone did.

Only later did I learn to call it what it was.

Pressure.

In the book, I acknowledged openly that I succumbed to peer pressure and did not follow my father's counsel.

That sentence is not a small admission. It is a confession of how strong the crowd can be.

When a boy is surrounded by age-mates, he does not want to be the one who stands out as afraid. He does not want to be laughed at. He does not want to be called a child when he is trying to become a man.

So, even if his father speaks wisdom, the boy may treat that wisdom as a delay. He may treat protection as an insult.

That is what I did.

And because I did it, I feel obligated to say something to those who come after me.

Peer pressure does not end after scarification.

It only changes its target.

A boy might be pressured into scars today.

Tomorrow he might be pressured into fighting.

The next day he might be pressured into revenge.

Later he might be pressured into corruption, into hatred, into following a leader blindly.

A crowd is a powerful thing.

If you do not learn how to resist the crowd early, you will follow it into places that destroy you.

So one of the biggest lessons of my scars is not about the scars alone.

It is about learning how to choose, even when everybody is shouting.

Section: A story inside the story

One of the reasons I have tried to tell this story with care is because scars are not only physical marks. They are also symbols that people load with meaning.

Some people treat the scars as proof of courage and pride.

Some treat them as a spiritual connection to ancestors and the unseen world, and they see the healing period as a time of introspection and connection.

Some treat them as tribal identity and rites of passage, and social standing.

These meanings are real in the minds of those who carry them.

But there is also another story inside the story.

It is the story of regret.

It is the story of a person who made an irreversible decision too quickly, and then spent years wishing life could be rewound.

In the file, there is a tale of Akech, a young man who begged for the marks, ignored warnings, and then was overwhelmed by agony and later plagued by remorse and regret.

Whether a reader takes that tale as a parable, a metaphor, or a literal story, the lesson is clear.

Some decisions feel exciting until they become permanent.

And when they become permanent, excitement can turn into regret.

That is why the same text urges the reader to learn from the mistake, to listen to the counsel of loved ones, and not to be blinded by curiosity or the allure of the unknown.

When I read those lines now, I hear my own father again.

And I hear my younger self again.

I hear the boy who wanted to be counted.

I hear the boy who feared mockery.

I hear the boy who was not yet trained in the courage of refusal.

Section: The world changed, and I had to change with it

One of the quiet pains of scarification is that it was designed for a certain world.

It was designed for a world where your community was your main universe.

A world where you lived and died among those who understood the meaning of the marks.

A world where identity was not questioned by global eyes.

But my life did not remain in that world.

Life carried me into other spaces.

And in those spaces, the marks were read differently, sometimes with curiosity and sometimes with hostility.

This is why the text itself asks the difficult question of how to balance pride in heritage with dignity and respect in a world that can discriminate and mistreat people because of difference.

The truth is that sometimes the world does not welcome difference.

It does not ask permission before it judges you.

121

It sees your face and makes assumptions.

And you have to learn how to live with that reality.

That is one of the reasons I came to believe that choice matters.

If a person chooses scars freely, with full awareness, he may be able to carry them with a stronger inner peace.

But if a person is forced, or mocked into it, he may carry them with bitterness, because he did not own the decision.

That bitterness can follow a person for years.

And bitterness is not a small thing. It can shape how a man treats others.

It can shape how he sees culture.

It can shape how he raises his own children.

So, again, choice is not a modern luxury. It is a moral requirement.

Section: The chapter I wrote to my daughter

There is one part of the file that always brings my heart into a different posture.

It is the section where I addressed my daughter directly, calling her "dearest daughter," and telling her that I had good news, that her brothers would be out of harm's way and would not suffer the same fate of facial markings.

I wrote that message with the tenderness of a father who wants his child to be spared.

I also wrote it with the vulnerability of a man admitting that what happened to him should not become a destiny for those who come after him.

In that same message, I said I wrote with her in mind, believing she would one day be mature enough to read and draw inspiration from the story.

That is the heart of why I kept writing, even when the story was uncomfortable.

Not to attack anyone.

Not to win a debate.

But to protect the next generation from repeating choices they did not have to make.

I also told her she was fortunate, like her brothers, that as a girl she would not have to withstand the worst of facial markings, and that the practice would not be encouraged when she grew into her teenage years.

Those lines reveal something important.

Even inside tradition, change is already happening.

Even inside communities that defend scarification strongly, there are shifts in attitude, especially as the world changes and health knowledge spreads and the future demands different kinds of preparation.

So that letter is not only emotional.

It is evidence.

Evidence that even within us, we know the cost, and we want our children to be safer than we were.

Section: The gift my scars gave me, and the gift they did not

I have said before that scars can give social recognition. They can give belonging. They can connect a person to heritage.

Those are real gifts, and I do not deny them.

But scars also did not give me what I truly needed.

They did not give me wisdom.

They did not give me a stable future.

They did not give me protection from violence.

They did not guarantee good character.

They did not prevent regret.

They did not stop me from being human.

In fact, my scars became one of the reasons I had to grow up in my thinking.

They forced me to confront the difference between what people praise and what truly builds a life.

When I was younger, I wanted a good name, and I thought scars would help me earn it.

Now I know that a good name is earned by integrity.

It is earned by restraint.

It is earned by responsibility.

It is earned by truthfulness.

It is earned by service.

Scars cannot do those things for you.

They can only sit on your forehead as a reminder that your character must become larger than your symbol.

Section: The nostalgia for a time when the practice had ceased

There is another line in the file that feels like a quiet confession.

It speaks about nostalgia for a time when the implementation of traditional practices such as scarification had already ceased.

That statement matters because it again proves what many refuse to admit.

The practice has not been continuous in the same way across all time. It has stopped in some periods and returned in others. It has shifted.

So the fear that questioning scarification will erase identity is not fully grounded.

Identity survived periods when the practice ceased.

That means identity can survive again.

So the question becomes not whether identity will survive.

The question becomes whether we will have the courage to protect children while preserving dignity.

In that same section, the text says that although we may lament the loss of certain practices, we cannot change history, and we should focus on the present and the possibilities it offers.

I agree with that.

I cannot remove my scars.

I cannot undo my choice.

But I can use my experience to guide someone else toward a better choice.

I can use my story as a small light, so that the next person is not walking blindly.

Section: What I want my readers to take, especially the young

If you are young and reading this, you might be standing at the edge of a decision.

Maybe it is scarification.

Maybe it is something else.

But the pattern is the same.

A crowd is calling you.

A father or mother is warning you.

Your friends are laughing.

Your heart is burning to be accepted.

This is what I want you to know.

The crowd does not pay the full price for your decisions.

You do.

Your body does.

Your future does.

Your mind does.

Your children might do too, if you carry bitterness and pass it down.

Listen to people who love you, not only people who want you to look brave in front of them.

If you choose a cultural practice, choose it with full awareness, not under threat of mockery.

If you refuse, refuse with respect, not with hatred for your own people.

You can respect your culture and still protect your body.

You can belong and still choose carefully.

You can honor elders and still ask honest questions.

This is not rebellion.

This is maturity.

Section: Closing of the chapter

I began this story as a boy who wanted to be seen.

I now end this chapter as a man who wants the next generation to be safer and wiser than I was.

I have written about scars, but I have also written about choice.

I have written about tradition, but I have also written about pressure.

I have written about identity, but I have also written about dignity.

And I have written about a father, because my father's love is one of the strongest truths in this entire story.

If this book helps even one young person pause before surrendering to the crowd, then my scars will have produced something better than pride.

They will have produced protection.

They will have produced wisdom.

They will have produced a future where belonging does not require injury.

CHAPTER 12: THE END OF THE KNIFE, THE BEGINNING OF RESPONSIBILITY

The place where a story must land.

Every story that begins with blood must end with meaning, or it will only be pain repeated in another form.

When I started telling this story, I did not begin with theories. I began with what happened. I began with the day my forehead became a public place. I began with the way peer pressure can drive a boy beyond his own wisdom. I began with the way a father can see danger before a son can see it. And I began with the truth that the body does not negotiate with pride, because I bled severely and appeared lifeless, unable to respond to people's questions.

But a story cannot land only on fear.

If it lands only on fear, it will become another weapon for those who want to insult a culture without understanding it.

If it lands only on pride, it will become another weapon for those who want to pressure children without admitting the risk.

So I want this ending to land on responsibility.

Responsibility is the only place where both truth and love can live together.

Section: The truth about what we are really defending

When people defend scarification, they often think they are defending culture. They think they are defending identity. They think they are defending a people's dignity against a world that laughs at African ways.

I understand that instinct. I feel it too.

But I have learned that sometimes what we defend is not culture itself. Sometimes what we defend is fear.

Fear of being laughed at.

Fear of losing unity.

Fear of change.

Fear of admitting that something we inherited can also harm us.

Fear of admitting that some practices were carried forward not only by meaning, but also by pressure and coercion.

The moment we admit that pressure exists, we become morally responsible for how we use it.

That is why many people refuse to admit it.

But I cannot refuse to admit it, because it is part of my story. I did not receive my scars in an atmosphere of calm freedom. I received them in an atmosphere where fitting in felt urgent, where the boy who refuses risks being treated as less.

So if we want to defend culture honestly, we must separate culture from coercion.

Culture can be celebrated.

Coercion must be resisted.

Section: Tradition can live without forcing the child

One of the biggest lies we tell ourselves is that a tradition will die if we stop forcing it.

If a tradition depends on coercion to survive, then it is already weak in its moral foundation.

A strong tradition can survive through teaching, through explanation, through voluntary commitment.

And our own histories prove that practices have changed over time. Even age-set patterns have shifted, including periods where scarification ceased, and later returned.

That means identity did not vanish when the practice slowed down.

It means culture did not collapse when the knife was not used.

So the fear that choice will erase us is not fully grounded.

What choice will do is remove bitterness.

What choice will do is reduce regret.

What choice will do is protect boys from being trapped in decisions they made mainly to silence mockery.

If a boy chooses scarification freely, with full understanding, then that is his choice.

If a boy refuses, and still remains respected, then the community has matured.

That is the measure of growth.

Section: The health truth we must stop avoiding

I also want to speak plainly about health, because I have seen how people treat health questions as insults.

The body is not an enemy of culture. The body is the place where culture is lived.

When you cut skin, you create risk. The text acknowledges pain and infections, and also recognizes the risk of transmission of HIV or Hepatitis B.

My own case proved the danger in another way. I lost a frightening amount of blood and appeared lifeless.

So when people speak about scarification, they must stop pretending risk is imaginary.

If the practice continues, then safety must become non-negotiable. The book mentions modern sterilization methods and disposable instruments as a way to reduce risk, while acknowledging that access and affordability can be difficult.

This is where responsibility becomes practical.

If you insist on the practice, do not insist on the old unsafe methods.

Do not insist on shared blades.

Do not insist on ignorance as if ignorance is purity.

A tradition that refuses safety is not protecting identity. It is protecting stubbornness.

And stubbornness is not a virtue when children's lives are involved.

Section: Alternatives are not an insult, they are a signal of care

Some people become angry when alternatives are mentioned, as if the suggestion is an attack.

But alternatives do not always mean abandonment. Sometimes they mean wisdom.

The text suggests that traditions can change with circumstances and that less invasive forms of expression, such as tattoos or piercings, may offer a way to express cultural pride with fewer risks.

I know some readers will reject that immediately.

That is fine.

But even if you reject the alternatives, do not reject the principle behind them.

The principle is simple.

We are trying to preserve meaning while reducing harm.

That is not betrayal. That is care.

And care is the real heart of any culture that claims to value human life.

Section: What I now understand about manhood

If I could go back and correct one idea in the mind of my fifteen-year-old self, it would be this idea: that manhood is proven mainly through pain.

Pain can test a person, yes.

But pain does not automatically produce wisdom.

Pain does not automatically produce integrity.

Pain does not automatically produce self-control in the deeper sense.

Sometimes pain produces pride.

Sometimes pain produces cruelty.

Sometimes pain produces bitterness.

Real manhood is proven through responsibility.

It is proven through restraint.

It is proven through truthfulness.

It is proven through protecting others, especially children.

I learned this lesson slowly, and I learned it through the same scars I once wanted to use as a badge.

For some time, I even felt disappointed that my scars were not as big as I had imagined. Then I learned the value was not in being grand, but in what the experience represented and the lessons it carried.

That is a shift from performance to substance.

That is the shift I want for our young men.

I want us to raise men who are proud of their identity, yes, but who are also mature enough to refuse harmful pressure.

I want us to raise men who can honor tradition without turning it into a weapon against other people.

I want us to raise men who can stand inside community without losing their ability to choose wisely.

Section: A final word to fathers, mothers, and elders

I cannot end this book without speaking again to the people who hold the strongest influence over children.

Fathers.

Mothers.

Elders.

If you read this story carefully, you will see something painful.

A father's warning is not always enough if the boy is surrounded by mocking voices.

My father warned me, and I still did it.

That means parents must not only warn. They must also protect.

Protection sometimes means removing the boy from the environment where the pressure is strongest.

Protection sometimes means speaking directly to elders and age-mates, and saying, this boy will not be mocked under my watch.

Protection sometimes means refusing to offer the child to the crowd.

And elders must remember this.

A child is not a tool for maintaining pride.

A child is not a sacrifice to prove identity.

A child is a life.

If elders truly love their community, they must treat children as future builders, not as materials to be used in social competitions.

Section: Why I wrote to my daughter, and why I wrote to you

There is a section in the book where I addressed my daughter and told her that I had good news, that her brothers would be out of harm's way and would not suffer the same fate of facial markings.

That message came from a father's desire to protect.

It also came from a man admitting that what happened to him should not become a destiny for those who come after him.

I wrote it believing she would one day be mature enough to read and draw inspiration from the story.

Now I say the same thing to every reader.

I wrote this so you can draw wisdom, not just emotion.

So you can think before you follow.

So you can choose before you surrender.

So you can protect your children before the crowd reaches them first.

Section: The balance I finally accept

I have asked hard questions, and I know hard questions make people uncomfortable.

But discomfort is not always disrespect.

Sometimes discomfort is the first sign that a mind is waking up.

The file itself asks the difficult question of whether we should abandon certain practices to avoid discrimination, or stand firm for recognition, and it says the challenge is balancing pride in heritage with dignity and respect.

That statement holds the tension well.

And here is the balance I finally accept.

We should not abandon ourselves to please the world.

But we should not harm our children to prove ourselves to the world or to ourselves.

We should preserve what gives life.

We should correct what takes life.

We should honor identity, but we should also honor health, freedom, and consent.

We should keep our history, but we should not worship it.

We should respect elders, but elders must also respect the child.

This is not confusion.

This is maturity.

Section: Closing of the book

My scars will not leave my face.

They will travel with me until I die.

But the meaning I attach to them can change, and it has changed.

At first, I wanted them mainly for belonging.

Now I want them to serve as a warning.

A warning about the power of peer pressure.

A warning about the danger of ignoring a loving father's counsel.

A warning about the reality of risk, because blood can flow beyond what pride expects.

And a warning that culture must never be used to crush the very people it claims to raise.

If you finish this book and you still love your culture, that is good.

If you finish this book and you still question some practices, that is also good.

But if you finish this book and you become kinder to children, more honest about pressure, more serious about consent, and more responsible about health, then this story has done what it was meant to do.

The end of the knife should be the beginning of responsibility.

CHAPTER 13: THE PEOPLE WHO HELD THE STORY

Why I am adding one last chapter.

I ended the last chapter with a clear closing, because the knife was the beginning of the story and responsibility became the rightful ending. But there is another truth that would make this book dishonest if I leave it unsaid.

No one writes a life alone.

Even when your story is personal, even when the wounds are yours, even when the blood that soaked the ground belonged to your body, the shaping of the story was never only in your hands.

A life is made in community. A book is also made in community.

That is why the original work included a dedication to my father and a full acknowledgement of the people who guided, mentored, corrected, and encouraged me.

In this Autobiography Series version, I want that spirit to remain alive, not as a formal ritual of saying names, but as an honest confession that my growth was never a solo journey.

Some readers may not care about this part. They want only events. They want only drama. They want only the scarification day and the consequences.

But I have learned that the most important part of any life story is not only what happened, but who stood near you while it happened, who tried to stop you, who lifted you after you fell, who challenged you when you were foolish, and who believed you could become more than the boy you used to be.

Section: The father whose counsel became a mirror

The dedication in the original text is simple, but it is heavy with truth. It names my father, Maluth Abiel Kueth, and it admits directly that his loving care shaped the person I became. It also admits that he advised me against receiving scarification marks, and that I ignored him because of peer pressure.

That is not just a dedication. That is a moral conclusion.

Many men talk about their fathers only when their fathers are no longer alive, and even then, they talk as if fatherhood is only about providing food, paying fees, or being strict. But a father's greatest gift is not money. It is counsel. Counsel is a lamp. It does not force you, but it shows you the edge of the cliff.

My father's counsel was the first lamp I refused.

Years later, it became the lamp that kept me honest. It is hard to lie to yourself when you remember clearly that someone tried to protect you, and you still walked into danger.

That is why I have said it again and again. Not because I enjoy repeating it, but because it is part of my redemption as a man. A man does not only move forward. A man also looks back and admits where he was wrong, so that his children do not repeat him.

If there is one thing I want every young reader to understand, it is this. A father's counsel is not an enemy of your freedom. It is often the oldest form of love.

Section: Mentors, elders, and the hands that shaped my thinking

In the acknowledgements of the original work, I named a mentor whose influence mattered deeply, Francis Ayul Nyok, and I recognized uncles and elders who contributed directly to the book, including Chol Deng Awuor, Achuil Nyok Lual, and Deng Akech Deng.

I want to pause here and explain why those names belong in the book, not only because they helped with writing, but because this story is rooted in an environment where elders matter. In our communities, elders are not only old people. They are living libraries. They carry the memory of customs, the meanings behind rites, the changes that happened quietly over time, and the reasons why certain practices persisted.

Sometimes youth treat elders as obstacles. Sometimes elders treat youth as threats. Both attitudes are destructive.

A healthy society requires a bridge between the living library and the new generation.

That bridge is mentorship.

Mentorship is when an older person does not only criticize you. He guides you. He answers your questions. He tells you the truth without humiliating you. He teaches you how to think, not only what to repeat.

That is what I received from those who were willing to invest in me. Their influence did not erase my scars, but it shaped the way I interpret them and the way I speak about them.

Section: Friends and companions who carried the writing process

The acknowledgements also list friends and supporters who helped during the writing process: Mut Peter Nyak, Elijah Kueth Malou, Gatluak Deng Reath, Eliza Ayak Ruei, and Puok Deng, among others.

People often imagine writing as a lonely art, one man with a notebook, sitting under a tree or at a desk, producing pages through sheer willpower.

But writing, especially autobiographical writing, is often emotionally heavy.

You relive things you would rather forget.

You reopen scenes you tried to bury.

You confront your own mistakes with no excuse left to hide behind.

In that process, encouragement matters.

A message matters.

A conversation matters.

A person who says, keep going, matters.

I know these things because I have lived them.

There were days I did not want to remember the shame of how pressure drove me. There were days I did not want to remember the blood loss and the moment I looked lifeless. There were days I did not want to feel again the regret of ignoring my father. There were days I did not want to carry the weight of being misunderstood by outsiders.

In such days, support is not decoration. It is oxygen.

So when I list those names, I am not doing a formal ritual. I am acknowledging oxygen.

Section: The sister-friend from Tanzania and the strange kindness of nicknames

One of the names in the acknowledgements that always makes me pause is Upendo, described as a good sister-friend from Tanzania who nicknamed me Gäärman.

That small detail may look minor to a reader, but it reveals something important about human life.

Sometimes the people who help you are not from your clan.

Sometimes they are not even from your country.

Sometimes they are people who meet you in a new phase of life and give you a kind of encouragement you did not know you needed.

A nickname can be foolish, playful, or deep. Sometimes it is a mirror. Sometimes it is a way of giving you a new identity when you are learning to exist beyond the narrow definitions of your childhood.

When a person from another place sees you and still chooses to give you affectionate language, it can soften the hardness you carry from a life of survival.

It can remind you that the world is not only danger.

It can remind you that human beings can be kind across borders.

That matters, especially for someone like me whose early life was shaped by fear, conflict, displacement, and the constant question of whether tomorrow would be safe.

So I keep that name in my heart as evidence that not all scars are on the skin. Some scars are in the mind, and sometimes kindness is one of the few medicines that can reach them.

Section: Why I wrote a message to my daughter

There is a section in the original text that is written directly as a message to my daughter, beginning with "Dearest daughter," and promising her that her brothers are out of harm's way and will not suffer the same fate of forehead scars. It says I wrote that section while she was only five months old, believing she would one day be mature enough to read and draw inspiration from the story.

That message is not only sentimental. It is a confession that a man's relationship with culture changes when he becomes a parent.

When you are young, you can treat risk like a game.

When you become a father, risk becomes personal in a deeper way.

You begin to see your children's faces inside every argument about tradition.

You stop talking as if "boys" are an abstract group.

You realize that "boys" means your own sons.

You realize that "girls" means your own daughter.

And once that realization settles in you, you cannot speak casually anymore.

That is why I wrote that message. It was my way of drawing a line between what happened to me and what I want for those who come after me.

It also says clearly that as a girl she would not be expected to endure the worst facial markings, and that the practice would not be encouraged when she grows into her teenage years.

That line reveals something else.

Even in communities where scarification is defended, many families already want change. They may not say it loudly, but they show it through what they choose for their children.

So the future is not fixed.

The future is being negotiated quietly in homes, in family conversations, in the private decisions of fathers and mothers who love their children more than they love public applause.

Section: The book as personal narrative, and the honesty of limits

In the abstract, the original text says clearly that although interviews were done, the book is not presented as a thoroughly researched account, and that it stands as a personal narrative of my life.

I respect that honesty, and I want it to remain in this rewritten version as well.

There is a difference between a personal testimony and an academic research project.

A testimony does not claim perfection.

A testimony claims sincerity.

It claims that the writer is telling what he lived, what he saw, and what he learned.

When a man speaks from testimony, he may not have every historical detail of the practice across centuries, but he can tell you the truth of how the practice operated in his environment, how it shaped his thinking, how it placed him under pressure, how it almost cost his life through blood loss, and how it changed his relationship with his father.

That truth matters.

And it is not small.

Because sometimes the most reliable truth is not found in a library, but in a wound that someone survived.

Section: Publication details as part of my journey

Even the publication details in the original file carry a story.

The work states it was copyrighted in 2013, and lists Discipleship Press, a website, an email address, and a phone contact, as well as a P.O. Box in Nairobi, Kenya.

Those are not merely administrative lines.

They represent a season of my life, a season when my writing was becoming more than private reflection.

They represent the reality that I have lived across places, that my growth and my storytelling have not remained locked in one village, and that my identity has had to negotiate between the old world and the new one.

When a person publishes, he is doing something risky.

He is placing himself in public.

He is allowing strangers to judge his private wounds.

He is also taking responsibility for the message he releases into the world.

So those publication lines remind me that this story was never meant to remain hidden.

It was meant to become a witness.

Not a witness against my people, but a witness for truth inside my people.

Section: The kind of gratitude that is not performance

Gratitude can be fake when it is used to impress people.

But gratitude becomes real when you acknowledge people who helped you become honest.

That is the most difficult kind of help, because honesty is expensive.

Many people will encourage you to be successful.

Fewer people will encourage you to be truthful.

Truth brings conflict.

Truth brings misunderstanding.

Truth brings criticism.

Truth brings loneliness at times.

So when I thank those who stood with me, I am thanking them not only for helping me write, but for helping me carry truth without collapsing.

Some of those thanked were elders who gave cultural knowledge.

Some were friends who supported the writing process.

Some were companions who simply believed I could tell this story in a way that serves others.

And my father remains central, because his counsel is one of the main moral lessons of the whole book.

Section: What I want the next generation to inherit from this book

If I had to name the inheritance I want to pass forward, it is not the scars.

It is not the knife.

It is not the performance of endurance.

It is the ability to choose wisely under pressure.

It is the courage to listen to a loving warning.

It is the maturity to respect culture without worshiping it.

It is the strength to ask questions without insulting elders.

It is the discipline to protect children, even if the crowd is loud.

In one part of the original work, the narrative voice challenges the reader with questions about whether to hide cultural practices to avoid mistreatment or to stand firm and fight for recognition, while urging balance between pride in heritage and dignity and respect.

That question is still alive today.

But I want to add something practical to it, because questions alone do not protect a child.

If you are a parent, do not outsource your child's future to peer pressure.

If you are an elder, do not use ridicule as a tool of culture.

If you are a young person, do not confuse mockery with truth.

If you are an outsider, do not confuse difference with primitiveness.

And if you are a reader who carries scars, do not use them as a reason to despise those who do not.

This is how I want the next generation to think.

Section: A final return to my daughter's message

I want to return one more time to the message written to my daughter, because it carries a tenderness that sums up the spirit I hope remains after the final page.

It says the brothers will not suffer the same fate, and it says I wrote with her in mind while she was very young, believing she would one day read and draw inspiration from it.

That is the heart of the Autobiography Series.

Not to worship the past, but to give the future a clearer road.

Not to glorify pain, but to transform pain into wisdom.

Not to attack identity, but to protect life while honoring heritage.

Not to win debates, but to raise human beings who can live with dignity.

Section: Closing of the chapter and the book

So this final chapter is my quiet bow to the people behind the story.

To my father, who warned me, loved me, and still remained my father even when I disobeyed him.

To the mentors and elders who guided the making of this work.

To the friends who supported the writing when the memories were heavy.

To Upendo, whose friendship and small kindness remains part of my human story.

To my daughter, whose existence changed the way I think about tradition and protection.

And to every reader, especially the young, who will one day stand at the edge of a decision and feel the crowd pressing in.

May you learn earlier than I did that belonging should never require injury.

May you learn earlier than I did that counsel is sometimes love wearing the face of refusal.

May you learn earlier than I did that your dignity does not need a blade to be real.

May you carry your culture with honor, but may you also carry your children with protection.

This is the end of my story on scarification, but it is not the end of my responsibility as a father, as a son, as a writer, and as a human being.

CHAPTER 14: THE QUESTIONS THAT FOLLOW A MARKED FACE

The questions that never stop.

After a while, you stop thinking of your scars as a fresh event and start experiencing them as a permanent invitation to questions.

Some questions come from curiosity.

Some come from judgment.

Some come from fear.

Some come from genuine respect.

And some come from people who do not know what to do with anything that does not match their idea of "normal."

What surprised me is that the questions did not only come from outsiders. They also came from my own people, from those who share the culture. Because even within the community, scarification is not one feeling and one opinion. It is many feelings living side by side.

The file itself shows that this topic is not settled, even among South Sudanese, because it records the continuing debate between those who defend scarification as heritage and those who condemn it on health and human rights grounds.

Once I understood that, I stopped trying to force a single answer on the subject. Instead, I began to collect the real questions that keep returning, and I began to treat them like a father treats a fire: not by pretending it is not hot, but by respecting its heat and keeping it from burning children.

Section: "Why did you do it if your father refused?"

This question lands hardest because it forces me to admit the simplest, most painful truth of the entire story.

My father did not consent. He advised me against it, and I still went ahead because I wanted to fit in.

When people ask me that question, I hear two things inside it.

146

One, they are asking about the power of a father's voice.

Two, they are asking about the power of a crowd.

And this is where scarification stops being only a cultural practice and becomes a lesson about human behavior.

A child's mind is still forming. His idea of dignity is often borrowed from the people around him. If the people around him say, "This is what makes you a man," he starts to fear the alternative. That fear can become stronger than family counsel. It can even become stronger than the instinct of self-preservation.

That is why the book warns about the consequences of social pressure and urges that the decision should be personal rather than driven by external pressure.

My answer to that question, today, is not an excuse. It is a warning.

If peer pressure could push me beyond my father's protection, it can push any boy.

So parents must not underestimate the crowd.

And boys must not underestimate how expensive it can be to buy belonging.

Section: "Did it almost kill you, or is that exaggeration?"

I wish it was exaggeration, because it would make the story easier to carry.

But it was not exaggeration.

I bled severely, and I appeared lifeless, unable to respond to people's questions.

People may not want to hear that detail because it disrupts the clean heroic picture. It introduces risk into a practice that many prefer to describe only as courage and pride.

But the body does not obey our preferred stories. The body tells the truth in blood.

And that truth matters for another reason.

If we hide the danger, we recruit the next generation using half-truths. We become sellers of a product called "manhood," and we hide the side effects.

That is not tradition. That is manipulation.

Section: "Is it really 'our' practice, or did it spread through outsiders?"

I have heard arguments that scarification was amplified by colonial systems, used as a method to separate groups, and I have also heard arguments that it existed long before and should not be blamed on outsiders.

I used to think that settling this origin debate would settle the moral debate.

It does not.

Even if a practice is indigenous, the moral question remains.

Does it still protect the child today?

Even if a practice is ancient, the moral question remains.

Is it carried by understanding, or carried by ridicule?

Even if a practice is part of identity, the moral question remains.

Can identity be preserved without coercion?

I no longer treat the origins debate as the main point. I treat it as one layer.

Because what harms children is not only origin. What harms children is enforcement.

Section: "Has scarification always been done the same way?"

This question matters because many people defend the practice using the phrase, "This is how we have always done it."

But the file itself shows that the practice has not been uniform across time and age-sets. It records that some age groups did not practice scarification, and later age groups adopted it.

That fact does something powerful.

It breaks the myth of unchanging continuity.

It means culture has already shifted before.

So when someone proposes change, it is not automatically betrayal. It can be a continuation of a long pattern of adjustment.

This is also why nostalgia appears in the text for a time when some traditional practices like scarification had ceased.

So I tell people this:

If the practice changed before, it can change again.

The question is not whether change is possible.

The question is whether we have the wisdom to guide change without insulting ourselves.

Section: "If you regret it, does that mean everyone regrets it?"

No. And this is where I have to be careful.

Because people try to use personal regret as a weapon.

Some try to use my regret to insult a whole culture.

Others try to silence regret to defend pride.

Both approaches are wrong.

The truth is that experiences differ. Even among scarred men, some carry their marks with pride, and some carry them with regret. The file includes a voice of a man who wished he could remove his scars, even though they were not very visible.

That single voice is important because it proves something many do not want to admit.

Not everyone experiences scarification as honor.

Some experience it as a burden.

So my regret does not cancel another man's pride.

And another man's pride does not cancel my regret.

What must be cancelled is coercion, because coercion is what turns a personal choice into a lifelong prison.

Section: "What about health, infection, and disease?"

This is the question many people avoid because it is uncomfortable, especially when tradition is treated like sacred ground.

But the text does not avoid it. It acknowledges pain and infections, and it also notes the risk of transmission of HIV or Hepatitis B.

It also discusses modern sterilization and disposable instruments as ways to reduce risk, while admitting that access and affordability can be hard in many areas.

When I think of this question, my mind returns to my own blood loss and the moment I looked lifeless.

So I answer it with a hard line.

If a community insists on continuing a practice that cuts skin, then safety must not be optional.

And if safety cannot be guaranteed, then pushing children into the practice becomes even harder to defend.

Section: "Should we hide our practices to avoid discrimination, or stand firm?"

This question shows up in the text as a direct challenge, and it admits there is no easy answer, because the real task is balancing pride in heritage with dignity and respect in everyday life.

I have lived that tension.

I know what it means to carry a face that is fully understood in one world and misread in another.

So I will say what I believe is the most honest position.

Do not hide your identity out of shame.

But also do not sacrifice children to prove identity.

Stand firm in what gives life.

Be flexible in what causes avoidable harm.

If we love our people, we should not demand blood from our children as proof of loyalty.

Section: "If scars are identity, what is identity without scars?"

This is where the deeper talk begins.

Because the truth is, identity is not only what is written on the skin. The text even describes scarification as a kind of "writing," with language that links the act to inscription.

But a person is also written by other things.

By language.

By values.

By how they treat elders.

By how they treat women.

By how they raise children.

By how they handle anger and conflict.

By how they serve community.

That is why I have said again and again: scars cannot manufacture character.

They can become a symbol, but symbols must never replace substance.

Section: The question I ask myself now

After all the questions people ask me, there is one question I ask myself.

If I could go back to that season, knowing what I know now, what would I want for that boy?

I would want him to have real choice.

Not choice in words, but choice in reality.

Choice without mockery.

Choice without exclusion.

Choice without being treated as less.

Because once you remove coercion, tradition can breathe.

And once tradition can breathe, it becomes a home again, not a trap.

That is what this chapter is for.

To place the questions on the table, not to end the book, but to prepare us for what comes next.

Because Part IV and Part V will move us from reflection into the living future: how these lessons continue shaping my decisions, my relationships, and my responsibility toward the next generation.

PART IV

CHAPTER 15: THE ROAD OF QUESTIONS AND THE PEOPLE I WENT TO MEET

Part IV begins with movement.

Part III was my wrestling with meaning. Part IV begins with movement.

A scar sits still on the face, but the questions around it do not sit still. They move with you. They follow you to school. They follow you to town. They follow you into church. They follow you into new friendships. They follow you into places where nobody shares your language. They follow you into places where your face is the first thing that speaks before you open your mouth.

So I reached a stage where I realized something simple.

If I wanted to speak about scarification responsibly, I could not speak only from my pain. I had to listen to other people's memories. I had to learn how different communities describe the same practice. I had to learn why some defend it strongly, why some regret it quietly, and why some have mixed feelings they do not know how to express without being attacked.

That is why this book included interviews, even while making it clear that it is not presented as a fully researched account.

I needed to talk to people, not to win arguments, but to understand the human side of what we often reduce to slogans.

Section: The year my scars met another road

I want to say this clearly because it explains the change that took place inside me.

My marks came at a young age, and later I walked into another kind of initiation, not with a blade, but with faith and conscience. The file connects my scarification experience to the season of 1997 and describes it as a time that also overlapped with my discovery of Christianity and dedication to its teachings.

That overlap matters.

When you meet God, or when you think you have met God, you start seeing your life with a different lens. You begin asking what is truly necessary. You begin asking what is truly good. You begin asking whether every inherited practice is automatically right simply because it has been inherited.

That does not mean you stop being who you are. It means you become more awake to the difference between culture as a home and culture as a chain.

So, in Part IV, I want to show how the scars did not remain only a childhood memory. They became a question that shaped my learning, my friendships, my faith, and the places I traveled to seek understanding.

Section: Why I chose interviews and conversations instead of only memory

Memory is powerful, but memory is also limited. It tells you what you lived, not what others lived.

When I started asking questions, I noticed that scarification is discussed in two ways.

One way is like a drumbeat. Loud. Proud. Certain.

Another way is like a whisper. Quiet. Careful. Mixed.

The loud way often speaks about identity, belonging, unity, and protection. The file describes how facial markings can represent lineage, tribe, and social standing, and how they have served as symbols of solidarity and belonging, even as protective markers in times of conflict.

The quiet way often speaks about health risks, infection, and social pressure, including discrimination against those without marks and the psychological weight that can follow.

Both ways are speaking about real experiences.

So I began to believe that if I only speak from my own story, I will miss something. I will miss the many voices that shaped how communities practice, defend, and question scarification.

That is why I went to people.

And that is why this chapter is about the road.

Section: The places where questions became real again

When you read a list of interview names and locations, it can look like a dry reference page. But for me, those lines are not dry. They are footsteps.

They show that I spoke with people across different parts of South Sudan and beyond, including Upper Nile locations, Nasir, Malakal, and also Goli in Yei River County at Emmanuel Christian Training Centre.

To someone who has never traveled those paths, the names might appear like simple geography.

To me, they are the names of places where people carry stories in their bodies.

Mataar, Upper Nile State.
Wunbut, Upper Nile State.
Abwong, Upper Nile State.
Nyongjok, Upper Nile State.
Nasir Town.
Malakal.
Goli, Yei River County at Emmanuel Christian Training Centre.

Each of these places carries a slightly different relationship to scarification, shaped by subgroups, history, conflict, and changing life patterns.

So when I say I went to listen, I mean I went to sit with human beings who are not paragraphs, who are not theories, who are not arguments, but people.

Section: The Emmanuel Christian Training Centre season

Some people may find it surprising that scarification conversations took me into a Christian training environment. But life does not separate itself into clean rooms the way books sometimes do.

A man can carry scars and still pursue faith.
A man can carry scars and still study Scripture.
A man can carry scars and still question what he inherited.

The interview list shows multiple conversations tied to Emmanuel Christian Training Centre in Goli, Yei River County, including interviews with Mut PN (21st February 2012) and Paul PM (23rd October 2011).

I want to tell you what that meant for me, not only as information, but as a turning point in how I carried my story.

In a cattle camp environment, scarification is treated as a social requirement. In a training environment where people speak about faith, character, and spiritual growth, scarification begins to sit beside other questions.

What is a man?
What does God require?
What is the value of the body?
How do we honor elders without surrendering conscience?
How do we handle identity without turning it into oppression?

These questions do not automatically erase tradition. But they force you to look at it carefully.

They force you to admit that not everything inherited is untouchable.

They force you to admit that choice matters.

And choice became a major theme in my later thinking about scars.

Section: The conversations that made me more careful with language

Sometimes the biggest damage does not come from a blade. It comes from a mistranslation.

The file warns about mistranslations and misunderstandings, giving an example of the Dinka term "muonyjang" being wrongly translated in a way that creates harmful stereotypes, and calling for accurate translation and open dialogue.

I include this in a chapter about my interviews because I learned that when people talk about scarification across languages and cultures, they often carry misunderstanding without knowing they carry it.

One person hears a word and turns it into an insult.

Another person hears a word and turns it into evidence that a whole people are backward.

Another person hears a word and turns it into a joke.

That is not harmless.

Language shapes how outsiders treat you, and how you treat yourself. If your identity can be mocked because someone mistranslated your words, then you begin to understand that scars are not the only issue. Communication is also an issue.

So my road of questions became also a road of learning how to speak carefully.

How to explain without provoking.
How to correct without shaming.
How to defend dignity without lying.

Section: The people behind the initials

When you read "Interview by author," it can sound distant. But those were real voices.

Gatluak DR, interviewed in 2000 in Mataar, Upper Nile State.
Kueth EM, interviewed in 2010 in Wunbut, Upper Nile State.
Puok DK, interviewed in 2003 in Nasir Town, Upper Nile.
Bol PL, interviewed in 2012 in Malakal, Upper Nile State.
Upendo N, interviewed in 2012 at Emmanuel Christian Training Centre, Goli.

Those names remind me that I was not only writing about myself. I was also entering a conversation that belongs to many people.

Some of them spoke like defenders.
Some of them spoke like critics.
Some of them spoke like tired men who do not want another fight, but still want their children to be safe.

I learned something important from this.

When a society is divided on a practice, the worst thing you can do is mock either side.

Mockery closes ears.

Mockery hardens hearts.

Mockery makes people defend what they might have corrected if approached with respect.

That is why I tried to make this book educational, not insulting. The text itself says the work aims to be a stimulating and educational companion rather than an encyclopedic account.

Section: The day I realized scars affect daily life in simple ways

There is a way scarification is discussed that feels too big, like it is only about identity and initiation. But scars also affect daily life in small ways.

The file notes that facial markings can convey information such as marital status, age, and level of education, shaping daily social interactions.

When I first read that line, I nodded, because it is true in many communities. People read your face quickly. They place you in a category. They decide how to approach you.

But then another thought came.

In modern settings, people can still read your face, but they may read it wrongly.

They may assume you are uneducated when you are educated.

They may assume you are violent when you are peaceful.

They may assume you are a problem before you have spoken.

So scars can become both a social passport and a social burden, depending on where you stand.

That is why Part IV matters. It is the section where the story moves into the wider world, where the same marks that create belonging in one place can create suspicion in another.

Section: The tension I carried in my chest

There were moments I felt proud.

There were moments I felt embarrassed.

There were moments I felt nothing at all, because scars can become normal to you until someone stares at you too long.

When I was younger, I wanted a good name, and I assumed scarification would help me earn social approval. The file describes this desire for a good name and reputation, and it also describes the disappointment that can happen when the scars do not match one's expectations.

That line about disappointment is not only about size. It is about the childish imagination of what scars will do for you.

A boy imagines scars will solve belonging.

A boy imagines scars will turn him into a man.

A boy imagines scars will shut the mouths of those who mock.

But later, the man realizes that scars do not solve the deeper human problems.

They do not solve fear.
They do not solve envy.
They do not solve hatred.
They do not solve tribal superiority.
They do not solve the hunger for dominance.

So I carried tension.

Part of me wanted to defend my people when outsiders judged us.

Part of me wanted to protect children from being pushed into irreversible decisions.

I did not always know how to hold both positions without being misunderstood.

That is why I kept walking the road of questions.

Section: Why I refused to treat health as an insult

When people are uncomfortable, they often call health questions a foreign attack. But disease does not ask whether you are defending culture or not. Infection does not wait for you to finish your debate.

The file speaks directly about health risks, including infection and complications due to lack of sterilization, and it also mentions risks of HIV or Hepatitis B transmission in such practices.

I do not mention this to scare anyone. I mention it because I have lived the reality of severe bleeding and collapse, and I know how quickly a body can become weak when a practice is handled carelessly.

So, as I traveled and talked to people, I became more convinced that if any community insists on continuing a cutting practice, safety must become a serious requirement, not an optional suggestion.

And if safety cannot be assured, then at minimum, coercion must stop. Because coercion plus risk is a cruel combination.

Section: The day I began thinking about solutions instead of only debates

At first, my mind was trapped in debate.

Is it good or bad?
Is it ours or foreign?
Should we keep it or abandon it?

But the more I listened, the more I realized that real life is not only debate. Real life is problem-solving.

The file speaks about the need for collaborative efforts to preserve heritage while minimizing negative consequences, including safer techniques, hygiene awareness, and fostering inclusive environments that challenge harmful stereotypes.

When I read that, I felt something settle.

This is where the conversation should go.

Not only toward defending or condemning, but toward protecting life while preserving dignity.

Not only toward shouting, but toward building.

This is also where Part IV begins to open into Part V later, because solutions are not only ideas. Solutions require community choices, parental courage, and a new definition of manhood that is not built on forcing children.

Section: The story of Upendo and the reminder that not all learning comes from your clan

The acknowledgements mention Upendo as a sister-friend from Tanzania who nicknamed me Gäärman, and they show that she also appears as an interviewee in 2012 at Emmanuel Christian Training Centre in Goli.

I want to pause on this for a reason.

Some people think identity must be guarded by staying only among your own. But life taught me that sometimes understanding grows when you speak with someone from outside your immediate cultural circle, someone who asks different questions, someone who hears your story without the same internal pressure.

A friend like that can help you become honest.

Not by insulting your culture, but by letting you hear yourself.

Sometimes a person from outside notices what insiders normalize.

Sometimes a person from outside can say, "You speak like someone who still carries pain," and you realize you have been calling pain normal for too long.

So the road of questions was not only a road through places. It was also a road through relationships.

Section: The message to my daughter as the hidden driver of this part

There is a reason the "Dearest daughter" message appears in the file, and it is not only sentimental. It reveals what was driving me quietly while I was collecting voices and writing.

The file says I wrote that message while she was only five months old, telling her that her brothers would not suffer the same fate, and that she, as a girl, would not be expected to endure the worst facial markings.

That message is one of the strongest reasons Part IV exists.

Because once you become a parent, your arguments are no longer abstract.

A father does not argue for pride alone. A father argues for the safety of his children.

So even as I listened to defenders of scarification, I kept hearing a father's voice inside me saying, do not let this become a destiny for your sons.

I kept hearing the memory of my own father warning me, and I kept feeling the weight of how I ignored him because the crowd was louder.

That is why I did not stop at my own story. I went to gather voices, because the next generation deserves more than a single man's memory. They deserve a wider view of what this practice means to different people, and what it can cost.

Section: Where this chapter leaves us

Part IV is the part of the book where scars begin to meet the wider world more directly.

It is where the boy's wound becomes the adult's responsibility.

It is where the private story starts to carry a public task: to educate, to correct, to protect, and to keep dignity intact.

I am not ending anything here. I am setting the stage.

Because the road of questions does not stop with interviews and references. The road continues into real life decisions, into how a scarred man is treated, how he is misunderstood, how he learns to speak for himself, and how he chooses what to pass to his children.

That is where Chapter 16 will take us.

CHAPTER 16: THE DAYS I LEARNED MY FACE HAS TWO MEANINGS

The village meaning and the outside meaning.

There are two worlds a scarred face lives in.

In one world, the marks are a language. They are read quickly, almost lovingly, the way elders read a familiar name. People can tell where you come from. They can tell your age group. They can place you in the family of the community without asking too many questions. The face becomes a kind of introduction.

In another world, the marks are not a language. They are a puzzle. Sometimes they are treated like a warning sign. Sometimes they are treated like a strange decoration. Sometimes they are treated like proof of ignorance. Sometimes they are treated like proof of violence. Sometimes they are treated like something nobody wants to ask about, yet everybody stares at.

I did not understand this difference fully when I was young. I assumed the meaning of the scars would remain stable wherever I went.

But life does not keep meanings stable.

Life changes meanings when you cross borders, when you enter classrooms, when you step into churches that are not yours, when you meet people who did not grow up with cattle camps and age-set talk, when you speak English to people who cannot imagine a boy being pressured into cutting his face, and when you realize that what feels normal in one place can feel frightening in another.

Part IV is the part of my story where that reality became practical. Not as an argument, but as daily life. And it forced me to grow in ways I did not expect.

Section: The day I understood the stare is also a question

At first, I thought the stare was simply rude.

Then I realized the stare is a question that many people do not know how to ask. It is also fear that many people do not know how to admit.

When a person looks at you and looks away quickly, they are often afraid of being seen as disrespectful.

When a person looks at you and keeps looking, they are often trying to make sense of something they do not understand.

When a person looks at you and smiles too hard, they are sometimes trying to cover their discomfort with friendliness.

When a person looks at you and avoids your eyes, they may be treating you as a threat.

And then there are those who look at you with ordinary calm. Those people are rare. They do not make your scars the main subject of the room. They treat you like a human being first.

I began to notice that my forehead could create an atmosphere before I even spoke. The marks were doing their own work, both good and bad, without my permission.

And I remembered something from the interviews and the wider discussion in the text. Facial markings can shape daily social interactions, and people read them as signals about age, status, and other social categories.

That truth helped me understand why the stare exists. People have been trained, in many places, to read faces.

But it also showed me something painful.

In modern settings, people can still read faces, but they can read them wrongly.

Section: The quiet cost of being misunderstood

Misunderstanding is not always loud. Sometimes it is silent.

It is a job you do not get, not because you are unqualified, but because someone decided your face looks "different."

It is a friendship that does not form, not because you are unfriendly, but because someone thinks your scars mean you are not educated.

It is a conversation that ends early, because someone assumes you are from "a dangerous place," and they do not want to be close.

It is a joke told near you, where people laugh and pretend it is not about you, but you know it is.

It is the way you are watched by security in certain places, as if your face itself is a weapon.

These things rarely appear in official stories, because they are hard to prove. But they shape a person.

They can produce anger.

They can produce shame.

They can also produce a strange kind of resilience, where you decide that your character must speak louder than your skin.

The file speaks about negative consequences such as discrimination and the psychological weight that can follow scarification, especially when people are judged or treated unfairly.

When I first began to experience these things, I did not have the language to describe them. Later, as I reflected and listened to other voices, I realized this is not only my issue. It is a shared human issue. Any visible difference can trigger judgment.

But in my case, the difference was not an accident of nature.

It was a decision shaped by pressure.

And that made the misunderstanding feel heavier, because the marks were not only something I carried. They were something I chose when I was too young to measure how far life can go.

Section: A marked face in a place of study

School has its own way of sorting people.

Not always by wisdom, but by symbols.

Some people assume that anyone from a rural background is automatically behind. Some people assume that modern education is the only measure of intelligence. Some people assume that if you carry visible cultural marks, you must be trapped in the past.

These assumptions are lazy, but they exist.

I remember entering learning spaces and feeling the need to "prove myself" more than others, not because my mind was weaker, but because my face was marked.

In some moments, this pressure pushed me into doing well. It became fuel. I would tell myself, I will not let them reduce me to a stereotype.

In other moments, it made me tired. Because always proving yourself is exhausting. You want to rest as a human being, not as a representative of a whole people.

The text warns about harmful stereotypes that can be fueled by misunderstandings and mistranslations, and it calls for accurate translation and open dialogue.

That line is not only about language. It is about how quickly people build stories about you when they do not know you.

So I began to train myself in a new discipline.

When I meet judgment, I do not answer it with anger first.

I answer it with clarity.

If someone asks respectfully, I explain.

If someone mocks, I keep my dignity.

If someone stares, I let my behavior teach them that a marked face can hold a calm mind.

This discipline did not come instantly. It came through many awkward moments.

Section: The strange moment when your own people also judge you

167

One of the things outsiders do not understand is that even inside our own communities, people can judge each other about scars.

Some men treat the marks as proof of superiority.

Some men treat those without marks as less.

Some treat those with lighter scars as "not fully committed."

Some treat those with heavy scars as "too traditional."

Some treat the whole practice as foolish.

Some treat it as sacred.

So even among your own people, your face can become a topic.

This is why I stopped using simple language like, "We all believe this," or "We all do that." Because it is not true.

The interviews and discussions in the text show the ongoing debate among South Sudanese themselves, including strong defenses of scarification as heritage and strong criticisms on health and human dignity grounds.

That debate is real. And because it is real, a scarred person can be judged from both sides.

Outsiders may judge you for having marks.

Insiders may judge you for questioning the marks.

So where does a man stand?

He stands on truth, even if both sides misunderstand him.

That is not an easy place to stand, but it is the only honest place.

Section: The body remembers, even when the mind tries to move on

There is another side to living with scars that is not social.

It is personal.

It is the body's memory.

Even after years, there are moments when I remember the day itself with a sharpness that surprises me. The blood. The weakness. The moment I seemed lifeless and could not respond to people's questions.

That memory can return unexpectedly. Not always as fear, but as a reminder that my body once paid a heavy price for a decision driven by pressure.

And the older I became, the more I understood that the body is not only flesh.

The body is part of a person's dignity.

That is why health discussions are not insults. They are responsibility.

The text speaks plainly about risks including infection and transmission of serious diseases, and it also discusses the need for hygiene and safer techniques.

When I carry my own memory of collapse and blood loss, these lines become more than theory. They become a warning.

Section: The spiritual turn that changed how I speak

There was a season in my life when faith began to shape my thinking more deeply. The file connects my scarification experience and its aftermath with my discovery of Christianity and dedication to its teachings during that period.

I mention this here because faith changed how I spoke about scars.

Before faith, my talk could easily become pride against pride.

One group defending.

Another group attacking.

Many voices shouting.

After faith began to settle in me, I started thinking less about winning and more about what protects life.

Faith did not make me hate culture. It made me examine culture with a conscience.

It made me ask, if something is done, is it done with love?

If a boy is pushed into it through ridicule, where is the love?

If a boy is denied full choice, where is the love?

If a practice carries health risk and the community refuses safety, where is the love?

Faith also made me calmer with people who judge me. Because when a person's identity becomes anchored in something deeper than public approval, the sting of people's eyes becomes less powerful.

Not painless, but less powerful.

Section: A marked face and the problem of translation

As I moved through places where people did not share my mother tongue, I learned that the marks are not the only thing that can be misunderstood.

Words can also be misunderstood.

And misunderstandings can become stereotypes.

The text gives an example of mistranslation creating harmful stereotypes and calls for accurate translation and open dialogue.

I began to see how easily outsiders can misunderstand our terms for manhood, for identity, for social roles, and then turn that misunderstanding into a broad insult against a whole people.

I also began to see how easily we can misunderstand each other across tribes and languages inside South Sudan itself, and how that misunderstanding can feed division.

So I started to treat language as part of the work of healing.

If I explain my scars, I must also explain the meaning behind them carefully.

Not as a defense of everything, but as a clarification of what is true.

And I must also correct what is harmful, even if it came from my own side.

Section: The temptation to hide, and the decision not to

There were moments when I wished I could hide my forehead.

Not because I hated myself, but because I was tired.

Tired of questions.

Tired of stares.

Tired of being reduced to a symbol.

Tired of people thinking they know my whole story because they saw my face.

But I also knew something.

If I hide, I allow shame to win.

And shame is a thief. It steals dignity even when you have done nothing evil.

So I decided, slowly, not to hide.

I will not use my face as a weapon, and I will not allow others to use it as a reason to erase me.

The file raises the hard tension of whether people should abandon or hide cultural practices to avoid mistreatment, or stand firm and seek recognition, and it speaks about the need to balance pride in heritage with dignity and respect in daily life.

This is where I landed.

I will not hide in shame.

But I will also not defend coercion.

I will carry my marks, and I will speak truth about how I got them.

That is my balance.

Section: The lesson that followed me into fatherhood

In earlier chapters, I spoke about the message written to my daughter, and how the reality of being a parent changes how you speak about tradition.

That truth continued to grow in me.

When you imagine your sons, you imagine their faces.

And when you imagine their faces, you begin asking different questions.

Will they be mocked if they refuse?

Will they be pressured into pain to prove they belong?

Will they be safe if they go through it?

Will they later regret it?

Will it limit them in a world where travel and schooling and work require meeting many kinds of people?

This parental thinking changed how I looked at my own scars.

My scars became less about me and more about what I can prevent.

This is why the text speaks about collaborative efforts to preserve heritage while minimizing negative consequences, including hygiene awareness and inclusive environments that challenge stereotypes.

A father who loves his children cannot treat this topic as entertainment or pride-talk. He must treat it as protection.

Section: The meetings that sharpened my thinking

The interviews listed in the work were not decoration. They were part of my education, part of my attempt to hear different voices and not speak as if only my experience matters.

Those conversations took place across different towns and settings, including in Upper Nile locations, Nasir, Malakal, and at Emmanuel Christian Training Centre in Goli, Yei River County.

I met people who spoke with pride.

I met people who spoke with regret.

I met people who spoke with anger.

I met people who spoke with calm reasoning.

And through those voices, I learned one painful truth.

Many of our arguments are not really about scars.

They are about belonging.

They are about fear of being erased.

They are about fear of being mocked.

They are about the trauma of conflict, where identity markers once served as protection or danger, depending on who found you.

So when a person defends scarification with heat, he may not be defending the blade only.

He may be defending his sense of existence.

This understanding made me more careful.

If you want to guide change, you cannot insult the people you want to guide.

You must respect their fear while still telling the truth.

Section: The new discipline I had to learn

Living with scars in mixed settings forced a new discipline on me.

The discipline of not reacting too quickly.

The discipline of explaining without begging for approval.

The discipline of holding pride without turning it into superiority.

The discipline of correcting wrong ideas without hating the person who holds them.

The discipline of refusing to let my scars become an excuse for bitterness.

Bitterness is easy. Discipline is hard.

But discipline is what builds a life.

In earlier parts of the work, scarification is described as training composure, endurance, and self-control, and those qualities are praised as part of a rite of passage.

I now see that these qualities can be redirected.

If endurance is trained, let it be endurance for education, for honest work, for rebuilding families, for resisting revenge.

If self-control is trained, let it be self-control that refuses tribal arrogance.

If composure is trained, let it be composure that listens and reconciles.

This is how a painful ritual can still produce a useful lesson, even if we later decide the ritual itself needs to change.

Section: What this chapter prepares us for

Chapter 16 is the chapter where the scars stop being only a memory and become a daily companion in new spaces.

It is where I learned my face has two meanings.

One meaning inside my people.

Another meaning outside my people.

And because those meanings can clash, I had to grow.

I had to learn how to speak.

I had to learn how to listen.

I had to learn how to protect the next generation.

Part IV will keep moving, because movement reveals more than reflection alone.

In Chapter 17, we will step deeper into the practical choices that came out of these lessons, including how I began thinking about what a safer, more humane future looks like without losing dignity.

CHAPTER 17: WHAT I CHOSE TO DO WITH THE LESSONS

A chapter about decisions, not opinions.

There is a stage in life when you get tired of repeating the same arguments. You begin to see that arguments can run for years and still produce nothing. People can shout in circles and call it loyalty. People can threaten each other and call it unity. People can refuse to listen and call it tradition.

But a life is not changed by arguments alone.

A life is changed by decisions.

Part IV is not only about me being seen in new places with an old face. It is also about what I did with what I learned. This chapter is not an academic paper. It is not a campaign speech. It is the record of choices I started making as a scarred man who did not want to raise children inside the same pressure that pushed him.

I had already admitted the most painful parts.

That my father advised me against scarification, and I ignored him because of peer pressure.

That I bled severely and appeared lifeless, unable to respond to people's questions.

And that this was not only a private matter, because it belongs to a wider debate inside our society about heritage, health, dignity, and human rights.

Now the question became simple.

If I know what I know, what will I do with it?

Section: The first decision was not to hate my people

This may sound small, but it is not small.

When a person is hurt by a cultural practice, the easiest reaction is hatred. Hatred gives you quick energy. Hatred makes you feel strong. Hatred makes you feel like you have escaped something. Hatred can also make you careless, because it convinces you that the whole people are wrong, and only you are right.

But I refused that road.

I refused it because it is dishonest.

It is dishonest because my people are not a single character. They are mothers and fathers, elders and youth, kind ones and harsh ones, wise ones and stubborn ones. It is dishonest because scarification itself is not held with one feeling by everyone. The writing recognizes this difference by showing both defense and condemnation, and by linking the debate to real fears about discrimination, dignity, and respect.

So the first decision I made was this.

I will speak truth without turning my pain into hatred.

I will name what is harmful without insulting the whole identity.

I will correct what I can without pretending I can erase the past.

This decision saved me from bitterness.

Bitterness would have made me loud, but useless.

Truth with restraint made me useful, even when some people disliked it.

Section: The second decision was to stop glorifying the blade

There is a way people tell the story of scarification that turns the blade into a sacred object and the blood into proof of greatness.

That style of storytelling is dangerous.

It hides the risks.

It recruits boys through pride.

It turns silence under pain into a competition.

It makes fathers feel pressured to offer their sons to the crowd.

It makes boys feel they must buy manhood with injury.

But I had lived the part of the story that does not look heroic when you say it plainly. Severe bleeding. Collapse. The frightening moment when people asked questions and I could not respond.

So I made a decision.

Whenever I tell my story, I will not glorify the blade.

I will describe the reality as it is.

Not to shame anyone, but to remove the lies that surround the practice.

If someone wants to defend scarification, let him defend it with full truth, not with half-truth.

If someone wants to choose it, let him choose it with full awareness, not with fantasy.

This decision changed how I spoke.

It also changed how some young people listened, because they realized that bravery is not the same as recklessness, and pride is not the same as wisdom.

Section: The third decision was to treat "choice" as a moral line, not a slogan

In many communities, people say, it is your choice, but they do not mean it.

They mean, you are free to choose, but if you choose the wrong thing, we will mock you, exclude you, and treat you as less.

That is not choice.

That is a trap.

The writing warns directly about social pressure and pushes the idea that the decision should be personal, not driven by external pressure.

So I drew a line in my own mind.

I will not support any environment that uses ridicule to push boys into scarification.

If a boy chooses it freely as an adult, that is his decision.

But if a boy is being pushed through mockery, that is coercion wearing a cultural mask.

And I do not accept that mask.

This decision also affected how I responded to people who wanted to use my scars as a weapon.

Some wanted to use my scars to pressure other boys.

I refused.

Some wanted to use my scars to insult those who still practice scarification.

I refused.

I kept returning to the same principle.

Consent matters.

A child deserves protection from the crowd.

Section: The fourth decision was to stop treating health talk as an attack

I noticed something strange.

In many debates, people will accept discussions about cattle disease, famine disease, cholera, malaria, and many other health issues. They will accept vaccination for children. They will accept medical treatment when a gunshot or spear injury happens.

But when it comes to scarification, some suddenly treat health talk as a foreign insult.

Yet the body does not change because you are defending culture.

The writing does not avoid this. It speaks about infection and complications, and it raises the risk of transmission of HIV or Hepatitis B.

It also speaks about modern sterilization methods and disposable instruments as ways to reduce risk, while admitting that access and affordability are hard in many places.

So I made another decision.

If I am asked about scarification, I will always include health.

Not to frighten people, but to protect life.

If a practice continues, safety must not be optional.

If a practice continues, shared blades must not be defended.

If a practice continues, hygiene must not be treated like weakness.

If a practice continues, adults must stop pretending infections are just a small issue.

Because I had already seen how quickly a boy's strength can be drained by blood loss.

When you have seen that, you cannot speak carelessly.

Section: The fifth decision was to speak carefully about language and translation

Another thing I learned while moving through different places is that scars are not the only thing that can be misread.

Words can also be misread.

The writing warns about mistranslations and misunderstandings, using an example of a Dinka term being translated wrongly in a way that fuels stereotypes, and it calls for accurate translation and open dialogue.

This became part of my practical choices.

When I speak about scarification to outsiders, I do not use careless language that makes my people look like monsters.

When I speak about scarification to insiders, I do not use careless language that makes outsiders look like enemies.

I try to explain.

I try to correct.

I try to remove stereotypes on both sides.

This decision came from survival as much as from morality.

Because in a country like ours, misunderstanding becomes conflict faster than we admit.

And a scarred face is already vulnerable to misunderstanding. It does not need extra misunderstanding created by careless speech.

Section: The sixth decision was to shift the focus from "Keep or Abandon" to "Protect and Preserve"

For years, the debate often sounds like a fight between two camps.

Keep it, because it is ours.

Abandon it, because it is harmful.

But when you listen to people deeply, you realize both sides are often trying to protect something.

One side is protecting identity and belonging.

The other side is protecting health and dignity.

The writing itself frames the tension as a difficult balance between pride in heritage and dignity and respect, rather than a simple yes-or-no.

So I began to use different questions.

How do we preserve meaning without coercion?

How do we protect boys from ridicule?

How do we reduce risk if the practice continues?

How do we create a space where a young person can refuse without being treated as less?

How do we teach manhood in ways that produce responsibility, not only endurance?

These questions changed the kind of conversations I had with friends, with elders, and with younger people.

Instead of shouting "keep" or "abandon," I would ask them about the child.

I would ask them about the pressure.

I would ask them about the health risk.

I would ask them about the regret many men hide.

I would ask them about the future.

Some people did not like that approach, because it removes the comfort of slogans.

But others began to think.

And thinking is where change begins.

Section: The seventh decision was to listen beyond my own tribe and region

Part IV already showed that I did not only sit with one group of people. The list of interview settings includes multiple places in Upper Nile, Nasir, Malakal, and also Goli in Yei River County at Emmanuel Christian Training Centre.

Those names matter because they represent my effort to hear more than one voice.

When you only hear your own group, you begin to think your group is the whole universe.

When you hear others, you begin to notice patterns.

You notice that many communities struggle with the same human problems, even if the rituals differ.

Pressure.

Shame.

Belonging.

Fear of being erased.

Fear of being judged by outsiders.

And fear of change.

So I decided not to speak as if my experience is the only truth.

It is my truth, yes.

But there are other truths, and I must respect them if I want to speak responsibly.

This decision also protected me from arrogance.

It is easy to turn pain into pride by becoming the loudest critic.

But listening keeps you humble.

Section: The eighth decision was to let faith sharpen my conscience, not erase my identity

The writing connects my scarification experience to a season when I discovered Christianity and dedicated myself to its teachings.

That part of my life did not remove my scars.

It did not remove my tribe.

It did not erase my history.

But it did change how I measured what is right.

It made me ask about love and harm.

It made me ask whether a practice is carried with care or carried with cruelty.

It made me ask whether elders are protecting children or using children.

It made me ask whether unity is being built by truth or by intimidation.

So I decided to let faith make me more humane, not more arrogant.

There is a kind of religious talk that insults culture and calls it darkness without learning anything.

I refused that too.

Because if faith makes you disrespect your own people, then you have not learned the heart of faith.

So my faith did not become a weapon against my culture.

It became a lamp that helped me see where culture needs mercy and correction.

Section: The ninth decision was to write and speak as an educator, not as a fighter

The original work describes itself as meant to be stimulating and educational rather than an encyclopedic account.

That line influenced my practical approach.

I did not want to become a man who only fights everyone.

Fighting can be addictive.

It can make you feel alive.

It can also make you useless, because people stop listening and only prepare their counterattack.

So I leaned into education.

Education means you present facts.

Education means you show both sides of a debate.

Education means you admit the limits of your account.

The writing admits that although interviews were conducted, the book is a personal narrative, not a thoroughly researched account.

That honesty became part of my style too.

When I speak, I do not pretend to know everything.

I speak from what I lived.

I speak from what I heard from others.

I speak from what I learned.

Then I invite people to think, not to worship my view.

This approach did not make everyone happy.

But it made many people less defensive, because they could see I was not trying to humiliate them.

Section: The tenth decision was about my own home

A man can write a book and still fail in his own house.

A man can debate culture and still be a coward when it comes to protecting his children.

That is why, for me, the most important decisions were not the ones made in public.

They were the ones made in private.

The writing includes a message to my daughter where I said I had good news, that her brothers would not suffer the same fate of facial markings.

That was not a poetic sentence.

That was a line drawn in my own family.

It was me saying, I will not allow the crowd to use my sons the way the crowd used my fear of mockery.

It was me saying, I learned the lesson late, but I learned it.

And it was me saying, my scars will not become a family curse.

If someone wants to call me weak for that, they can.

But they will not pay the price if my child bleeds.

I will.

And I have already seen what severe bleeding can look like.

So my home decisions became the strongest proof that I was not just talking.

Section: The eleventh decision was to accept that some people will misunderstand me

Once I started speaking about choice, pressure, and safety, I began to be misunderstood from both sides.

Some defenders of scarification heard me as an enemy of culture.

Some critics of scarification heard me as too soft.

Some outsiders heard me as defending harm.

Some insiders heard me as insulting elders.

That is what happens when you refuse extreme positions.

The writing itself shows why this misunderstanding happens by reflecting the tension between preserving heritage and minimizing harmful outcomes, including stereotypes and discrimination.

So I decided to accept misunderstanding as part of the road.

If I keep my conscience clean, misunderstanding is not the end of my life.

But if I lie to please one side, then I lose myself.

So I accepted the burden of being misread at times.

I also learned a quiet discipline.

When people misunderstand you, do not rush to insult them.

Clarify.

Correct.

Then move on.

Some people will never be convinced.

That is fine.

The goal is not to win everyone.

The goal is to protect children and keep dignity intact.

Section: The twelfth decision was to keep asking the child-centered questions

Whenever the debate becomes too loud, I return to the simplest questions.

Is the boy being pushed by mockery?

Is the boy fully informed?

Is there medical safety?

Is there a clean instrument?

Is there a plan for infection?

Is there consent?

Is there a way to refuse without being treated as less?

If people can answer these questions honestly, the conversation becomes serious.

If people cannot answer them, then the debate is not about culture. It is about pride.

Section: Where this chapter leaves us

Chapter 17 is the chapter of practical choices.

It is me moving from regret into responsibility.

It is me refusing hatred, refusing the glorification of the blade, and refusing the lie that coercion is the same as tradition.

It is me accepting that identity does not have to be defended by hurting children.

It is me treating health as responsibility, not as insult.

It is me learning to speak carefully so that mistranslation and misunderstanding do not turn into stereotypes and conflict.

And it is me bringing the debate home, because the strongest proof of your beliefs is how you protect your own children.

Part IV is still moving.

In Chapter 18, we will go deeper into how these decisions affected my relationships and my standing among people, especially when I refused to let shame and pressure run my life again.

PART V

CHAPTER 18: THE KIND OF PEACE I WANTED AFTER THE SCARS

Part V begins with the future, not the knife.

Part V is where I stop speaking like a boy who survived something, and start speaking like a man who must build something.

A scar can be an ending for a careless mind. It can become the excuse a person uses to stop growing. Some people carry a mark and decide the story ends there, as if the mark is the final proof of identity, the final proof of manhood, the final proof of belonging.

But that is not how my life unfolded.

My scars were not the end of my journey. They were a beginning of questions that would not leave me alone.

Part IV ended with decisions. Part V begins with consequences and direction.

When you decide to tell the truth, you pay a price.

When you decide to protect children from pressure, you pay a price.

When you decide not to glorify pain, you pay a price.

When you decide to respect culture while still correcting what is harmful, you pay a price.

I learned this price in the ordinary ways of life, and I also learned it in the way people reacted to my words, my choices, and the stand I began to take inside my own home.

Section: The peace I wanted was not silence

Some people think peace means silence.

They think peace is when nobody talks about the problem.

They think peace is when the young stop questioning.

189

They think peace is when elders are never challenged.

They think peace is when the community looks united in public, even if fear is operating in private.

That is not peace.

That is pressure dressed like peace.

I grew up around pressure. I know how it looks when it pretends to be normal life. I know how it pushes boys into decisions. I know how it makes a father's counsel look like weakness, and how it turns the crowd into the true parent. I confessed clearly that I did not follow my father's counsel, and that peer pressure drove me into receiving the scars.

If that pressure can override a father's love, then a society that calls it peace is lying to itself.

So I began to define peace differently.

Peace is when a boy can refuse a practice without being mocked.

Peace is when a boy can choose a practice without being forced.

Peace is when a mother does not fear that her child will be used as a public trophy.

Peace is when elders do not rely on humiliation to maintain customs.

Peace is when culture is carried by understanding, not by fear.

That is the peace I wanted.

Not silence, but safety.

Not uniformity, but dignity.

Not intimidation, but belonging.

Section: The moment I stopped wanting to "win" and started wanting to "protect"

When you are young, you want to win. You want to be right. You want your voice to sound louder than others. You want to prove something.

But after the scars, after the blood loss, after the moment when I appeared lifeless and could not respond to people's questions, the desire to win began to feel childish.

I had seen how quickly pride can become danger.

So I stopped asking, how do I win this debate?

I started asking, how do we protect children and still keep our dignity?

That shift changed everything.

It changed how I listened to defenders of scarification.

It changed how I listened to critics of scarification.

It changed how I spoke to outsiders who mocked us.

It changed how I spoke to insiders who demanded obedience.

It also changed what I considered "strength."

Strength was no longer a boy staying silent under a blade.

Strength was a father standing between his child and pressure.

Strength was a community refusing to use ridicule as a tool.

Strength was an elder choosing wisdom over stubborn pride.

Strength was a young man refusing a harmful pattern even when his friends laughed.

That is the kind of strength that creates peace.

Section: The peace that starts in the home

I learned something that many public speakers avoid admitting.

Most cultural fights are not solved in conferences.

They are solved in homes.

The file contains a message I wrote to my daughter, telling her that her brothers would not suffer the same fate of facial markings, written when she was only five months old, with the hope that she would one day read and draw inspiration from it.

That message was not a poem. It was a decision.

It was me choosing what kind of father I wanted to be.

It was me refusing to allow the crowd to claim my children the way it claimed my fear of mockery.

It was also me admitting something important.

A man can be proud of his heritage and still decide that a certain practice should not touch his sons.

That is not betrayal.

That is fatherhood.

Some people want to treat fatherhood as only providing food, paying school fees, and being stern. But fatherhood is also protection, even when protection makes you unpopular among those who want to maintain old pressure patterns.

This is where the peace I wanted became personal.

I did not want to build a "public opinion" that sounded intelligent while my children suffered the same fate I suffered.

I wanted to build a future where the child's dignity comes first, and where culture can still live without demanding blood.

Section: The peace that includes honest health talk

Many people want cultural talk without health talk.

But the body is not an enemy of culture. The body is the place where culture lives.

The file speaks about risks including infection and the potential transmission of HIV or Hepatitis B. It also mentions modern

192

sterilization methods and disposable instruments as ways to reduce risk, while acknowledging the challenges of access and affordability.

When I read those lines, I cannot treat them as theory, because I remember my own severe bleeding and collapse.

So, the peace I wanted included the freedom to speak about health without being accused of hating the culture.

A culture that cannot listen to health warnings is not strong. It is defensive.

A community that shames people for discussing safety is not united. It is afraid.

Real peace includes the courage to protect life.

Real peace includes admitting that some practices carry risks.

Real peace includes building safer alternatives where possible, or at least removing coercion when safety is not assured.

So, when I speak about scarification today, I do not separate it from health. If someone insists on the practice continuing, then I insist that safety must not be optional. And if safety cannot be assured, then at minimum, the crowd must stop pushing children into it.

Section: The peace that can survive disagreement

One thing I noticed while collecting voices and listening across places is that disagreement is normal.

Some people defend scarification as heritage, identity, and belonging. Others condemn it because of health concerns and human dignity. The file records this ongoing debate among South Sudanese themselves.

Many communities treat disagreement as a threat.

They want one voice.

They want one position.

They want one posture.

But one voice is not always unity. Sometimes one voice is fear.

So the peace I wanted had to include room for disagreement without humiliation.

Room for elders to speak without being mocked.

Room for youth to question without being crushed.

Room for families to decide what is best for their children without being threatened.

That kind of peace is hard to build because it requires discipline.

It requires people to stop using shame as a weapon.

It requires people to stop treating every question as rebellion.

It requires people to stop treating every defense as backwardness.

This is why I began to value education more than fighting. The file frames the work as stimulating and educational rather than an encyclopedic account.

Education creates room for disagreement that does not become hatred.

Education allows the community to examine itself without feeling attacked.

Education helps the young to think, and helps elders to be heard, and helps outsiders to understand without mocking.

That kind of education is part of peace.

Section: The peace that corrects stereotypes, not only scars

I also learned that scars are not the only thing that harms us.

Misunderstanding harms us.

Mistranslation harms us.

The file warns about mistranslations and misunderstandings and calls for accurate translation and open dialogue, using an example of a term being wrongly translated in a harmful way.

This matters because a community can decide to keep or abandon scarification, but if outsiders still misunderstand its people, discrimination can continue in other forms.

So I began to pay attention to language.

How do we describe our practices?

How do we explain our words for manhood, identity, and belonging?

How do we correct outsiders who treat our marks as proof that we are less human?

How do we correct insiders who treat outsiders as permanent enemies?

How do we keep dignity while still being honest?

This is part of the peace I wanted.

A peace where our people are not reduced to stereotypes by careless translation.

A peace where we are able to explain ourselves without begging for approval.

A peace where our own words do not become weapons against us.

Section: The peace that comes from listening across places

Part IV showed that I did not stay inside one location when gathering voices. The interview references include Upper Nile locations, Nasir Town, Malakal, and Goli in Yei River County at Emmanuel Christian Training Centre.

Those place names matter because they remind me that human life is larger than one community's assumptions.

When you stay in one place, the pressure feels like law.

195

When you move through different places, you realize that what one group treats as unquestionable can be questioned elsewhere, and life does not collapse.

That is how the mind becomes freer.

That is how peace grows, because peace cannot grow in a mind that is trapped.

The road taught me that identity can be held without cruelty.

The road taught me that belonging can be built without humiliation.

The road taught me that a community can keep its pride without demanding blood.

The road taught me that change is not always betrayal.

Even the file's historical notes show that scarification practices have shifted across time and age sets, with some age groups not practicing it and later ones adopting it.

So, the peace I wanted was not the peace of a frozen culture.

It was the peace of a culture that can adjust, learn, and protect life while preserving dignity.

Section: The peace that honors my father's love

There is a reason my father remains central in this story.

The dedication names him, and admits that his loving care shaped me, and that he advised me against scarification, but I ignored him because of peer pressure.

A father's counsel is often the first line of peace in a child's life.

When a father warns, he is trying to prevent regret.

When a father resists pressure, he is resisting a community habit that can harm his child.

When I ignored my father, I did not only disobey him. I stepped out of the shelter of a love that was trying to protect me.

The peace I wanted later included honoring that love.

Not by repeating words, but by doing what I should have done earlier: listening.

So, even though I cannot reverse my scars, I can reverse the pattern.

I can become the father I needed.

I can become the adult who stands where my father stood.

I can become the one who is willing to be unpopular for the sake of a child.

That is part of peace too.

Peace is not only between tribes and communities.

Peace is also between a father and a son.

Peace is also inside the conscience of a man who admits he was wrong.

Section: The peace that does not shame scarred men

There is another danger I had to avoid.

When a person criticizes scarification, it can quickly turn into shaming scarred men, as if they are victims of stupidity.

That is cruel.

Most scarred men did not cut themselves.

Many were pressured.

Many were young.

Many were trapped between belonging and mockery.

So when I speak, I refuse to shame scarred men.

I also refuse to allow scarred men to shame unscarred boys.

The file includes a voice of a man who wished he could remove his scars, even though they were not very visible.

That line matters because it shows the quiet regret that many carry.

So the peace I wanted included compassion.

Compassion for the scarred man who is tired of judgment.

Compassion for the unscarred boy who is tired of pressure.

Compassion for the father who is trying to protect his child while still respecting elders.

Compassion for the elder who fears cultural loss, even if he is wrong in how he enforces the practice.

Compassion does not mean we accept harm.

It means we correct harm without turning people into enemies.

Section: The peace that puts the child at the center

Every time the debate becomes complicated, I return to the child.

A child is not a symbol.

A child is a life.

A child is a future builder.

A child deserves consent to be real, not a false "choice" guarded by ridicule.

The file itself pushes the idea that the decision should be personal and not driven by external pressure.

That is the moral center for me.

If the community can guarantee real choice, the conversation changes.

If the community cannot guarantee real choice, then what it calls tradition is often pressure.

So the peace I wanted is a peace where children are protected from public humiliation.

A peace where elders teach, not threaten.

A peace where manhood is trained through responsibility, not forced pain.

A peace where a boy can belong because of character, not because of injury.

Section: The peace that comes with faith and conscience

The file connects my scarification experience with a season of discovering Christianity and dedication to its teachings.

Faith did not erase my cultural identity, but it sharpened my conscience.

It made me ask whether love is present in the way we enforce a practice.

It made me ask whether we are protecting children or protecting pride.

It made me ask whether we are using culture as a home, or using culture as a tool to control people.

It also made me think about what kind of legacy I want to leave.

Because faith, at its best, forces you to think beyond your own comfort.

It forces you to think about the weak.

It forces you to think about children.

It forces you to think about the kind of society you are helping to build.

So my idea of peace became tied to conscience.

Not conscience that insults elders, but conscience that refuses cruelty.

Not conscience that despises culture, but conscience that protects life.

Not conscience that only criticizes, but conscience that also builds.

Section: What Part V will keep doing

Chapter 18 is the opening of Part V, and it sets the direction.

Part V will keep moving through the consequences of my choices, how people responded, how relationships changed, how I carried my scars in public spaces, and how I began to think about legacy.

I am not writing this as a conclusion.

I am writing it as a doorway into what comes next.

Because peace is not an idea that appears fully formed.

Peace is built over time.

Peace is built through repeated choices.

Peace is built when you refuse to hand your children to pressure.

Peace is built when you can disagree without humiliating each other.

Peace is built when you tell the truth without hatred.

Peace is built when you protect life and still carry dignity.

That is the peace I wanted after the scars.

CHAPTER 19: DEAREST DAUGHTER, THIS IS WHAT I PROMISED

Section: The chapter begins with a letter I wrote before you could read

I did not write Part V as a debate with anyone. I wrote it as a conversation with my blood.

There is something powerful about addressing a child directly. A child does not care how polished your arguments are. A child does not reward you for sounding clever. A child only carries one question in the eyes, even when they cannot speak it yet.

Are you safe with me?

In the manuscript, there is a section titled "PREDICTIONS" and it begins with the words "Dearest daughter," and I want to admit something that may surprise a reader who expects a cultural book, or a history book, or a book of interviews.

That section was not written for the crowd.

It was written for you.

I wrote it while you were still too young to understand any of this, while you were only five months old. I was writing about scars, but I was also writing about inheritance. Not cows, not names, not clan pride. I was writing about what kind of pain I would pass down, and what kind of pain I would stop with my own hands.

So let me return to that letter, not as a quote, but as a living memory that guides this chapter.

Section: "I have great news" was not a sentence, it was a decision

In that letter, I told you I had great news.

It was not the kind of news people celebrate with songs. It was not a political announcement. It was not a church announcement.

It was a father making a line in the sand.

I told you your brothers were out of harm's way and would not suffer the same fate as I did, marked with scars on the forehead.

Some people might read that and think it is simply a father's emotional statement. But I know what it means to make that statement in a society where pressure can become a law without being written.

When I was a boy, I did not stand strong enough to resist mockery. I followed the pull of young voices. I listened to the crowd instead of listening to my father. I said it plainly elsewhere in the manuscript: I ignored my father's wise counsel because of peer pressure.

That is why the letter matters.

It is a confession and a correction in the same breath.

It is me saying: I failed once, but the failure will not become a family curse.

Section: I wrote to you because I needed a witness

Why did I write it down?

Why not just decide quietly and move on?

Because I have seen how a quiet decision can be swallowed by a loud community.

In many of our societies, what is not spoken can be treated as nonexistent. What is not written can be denied later. A man can change his mind in public because it is easier than standing alone.

So I wrote to you as a witness.

I wrote it with you in mind, even while you were still a baby. I wanted the words to outlive my mood. I wanted a future version of you to look back and know what your father stood for, even before you could speak your first full sentence.

And I tied it to something deeper than emotion. I tied it to faith. I wrote that I held firm to my faith and believed you would one day be mature enough to read the story and draw inspiration from it.

People may disagree with me about scarification. They may argue culture. They may argue identity. They may argue pride.

But few people can argue with a father's responsibility.

A father must protect. If he cannot protect, then he should not ask for respect.

Section: What I meant when I said "harm's way"

"Harm's way" is not only the knife.

"Harm's way" is also the humiliation that forces a child into a decision.

"Harm's way" is the crowd that laughs at a boy until he obeys.

"Harm's way" is the belief that manhood is proven only by blood.

When I wrote that your brothers were out of harm's way, I was saying that I would not allow the old pressure to enter my home.

Some people think pressure is small, that it is just talk. But talk can be a weapon. Talk can be a whip. Talk can be the reason a boy walks toward pain pretending it is courage.

I know this because I lived it.

So the harm I wanted to block was physical, yes, but it was also psychological and social.

I wanted my sons to learn courage without being bullied.

I wanted them to be accepted without needing to bleed for acceptance.

I wanted them to understand heritage as a home, not a trap.

Section: "You are equally fortunate" and what that reveals about gender

In the same letter I told you that you too were fortunate, like your brothers. I told you that as a girl you would not have to withstand the worst of facial markings, and that it would not be encouraged when you grew into a teenager.

That sentence exposes something we do not always admit openly.

Many of our cultural burdens are carried differently by boys and girls.

Sometimes society protects girls from certain forms of pain but burdens them in other ways.

Sometimes society burdens boys with the idea that pain is the entry ticket to respect.

In my case, facial scars were tied strongly to male identity and male acceptance.

So when I told you that you would not have to face that, I was speaking truthfully about one thing, but I was also warning myself about another.

If I can protect you from one practice, then I must also be alert to the other kinds of pressure that come for girls: early marriage pressure, silence pressure, obedience pressure.

Part V is not only about scars. It is about every way society tries to claim our children.

Section: The year 2012 and why timing matters

I told you that you were lucky to read a book written by your loving and vulnerable dad back in 2012.

That year matters to me for a reason.

It reminds me that a man can be young enough to still be healing from old wounds, but old enough to stop passing them down.

It reminds me that fatherhood is not only biology. Fatherhood is a moral shift.

It also reminds me that writing is not just art. Writing is a tool for stopping generational repetition.

That is why the manuscript, even when it talks about language and culture, also speaks about autobiography as a way to preserve legacy and link generations.

People may think an autobiography is self-centered.

But for me, autobiography became the opposite.

It became my way of serving the future.

Section: The kind of man I became after the scars

Before the scars, I wanted to be accepted.

After the scars, I wanted to understand.

After I began to understand, I wanted to protect.

Protection looks different when you are no longer trying to impress your peers.

It looks like saying no.

It looks like being misunderstood.

It looks like being labeled proud, or Westernized, or disloyal.

But if protecting your children makes you unpopular, then popularity is not worth having.

This is one reason I keep returning to the memory of my father, because he is a model of the kind of man I needed to become. My father, Maluth Abiel Kueth, advised me against receiving scars, and I did not listen.

Now I have children.

Now the lesson is not theoretical.

Now I must do what he tried to do for me.

Section: A home that does not worship scars

There are homes that worship scars.

Not with songs, but with attitudes.

They treat scars as the proof of value.

They treat unscarred boys as incomplete.

They treat scars as a passport to respect.

I refuse that kind of home.

I do not deny the cultural story. I do not mock the elders. I do not spit on heritage.

But I also do not worship pain.

If scars happen, they happen. They become part of a man's history.

But they are not the measuring stick of a man's dignity.

This is why I wrote that letter to you with tenderness, not with pride. I wanted you to see the scars as something your father lived through, not something your brothers must chase.

Section: The truth about tradition is that it has changed before

One reason people fear reform is because they imagine tradition as a stone.

But tradition has moved before.

In the manuscript, when I discuss age-sets among the Ngok Dinka and note that earlier age-sets did not practice scarification, and later ones adopted it, the point is not to shame anyone. The point is simple: communities have adjusted their practices before, sometimes by choice and sometimes through influence.

So when someone tells me, "It must be done because it has always been done," I hear a sentence that history does not support.

And when I remember that, the fear reduces.

Because if our fathers adapted in the past, then we too can adapt now, especially when children's wellbeing is at stake.

Section: A letter is also a warning to my future self

A man can write something true today and become weak tomorrow.

That is why I wrote the letter.

It is a reminder to the future version of me who might get tired, who might want to avoid conflict, who might want to surrender to social pressure.

It says: remember what you promised when your daughter was five months old.

It says: do not become the kind of father who speaks courage and lives compromise.

It says: do not become the kind of man who criticizes pressure in public but obeys it in private.

It says: if your children trust you, do not trade that trust for community applause.

Section: Why I still speak with respect

Even as I draw a line for my children, I still speak with respect toward those who hold the practice as sacred.

Because insults do not build a better future.

Because humiliation is the same weapon that pushed boys like me into scars.

Because if I want a society that stops forcing children, then I must stop forcing adults through shame.

So I choose words carefully.

I speak firmly, but I do not mock.

I disagree, but I do not dehumanize.

I argue, but I do not turn relatives into enemies.

This is not weakness.

This is discipline.

Section: What Chapter 19 adds to Part V

Chapter 18 opened Part V by describing the peace I wanted after the scars.

Chapter 19 makes that peace concrete.

It shows that peace is not only a public idea.

Peace is a promise made in a small family space, a promise carried through time.

Peace is a father writing to his daughter, saying: my pain will not become your inheritance.

And the reason I can speak like this without fear is because I know what writing can do.

Writing preserves memory.

Writing becomes a bridge.

Writing makes a promise harder to erase.

That is why I wrote the letter, and that is why I am placing it at the center of this chapter.

Because one day, you will read it, and you will know that your father did not only survive the scars.

He learned from them.

CHAPTER 20: WHEN THE STORY LEFT MY HANDS

Section: There is a moment when your story becomes public

A man can live through pain and still keep it private.

He can tell the story to himself, in his mind, in the silence of night. He can tell it to a friend by the fire. He can tell it in short pieces, laughing to hide the weight. He can also bury it, pretending it never happened, while his body remembers every drop of blood.

But there comes a moment when the story refuses to stay inside you.

That moment is not only emotional. It is practical.

It happens when you realize that your personal memory has become a public pattern.

It happens when you see younger boys standing where you once stood.

It happens when you notice the same pressure, the same ridicule, the same fear of being excluded, moving through the next generation like a wind that never stops.

And it happens when you become a father and the question changes from "What happened to me?" to "What will happen to my children?"

By the time I reached that stage, the scars were no longer only scars. They were a warning sign on my own forehead, and I needed to decide whether to keep that warning in my head or release it into the world as a message.

That is what this chapter is about.

It is about the moment the story left my hands.

Section: Why I did not write to impress anyone

If I wanted to impress people, I would have written a proud book. I would have painted myself as a hero. I would have turned the blade into poetry. I would have made the scars sound like a crown.

But this story was never written to impress.

It was written to tell the truth that many people avoid because it makes everyone uncomfortable.

The truth that peer pressure can override a father's counsel.

The truth that blood loss is not a small detail, and that I reached a moment when I appeared lifeless and could not even respond to questions.

The truth that our society is not united in one opinion about scarification, and that there is a real debate among our own people, with strong defenses and strong criticisms tied to health and human dignity.

I did not write as a judge looking down on others.

I wrote as a witness describing a human pattern.

Section: The hardest part was admitting my own weakness

Many readers can accept that a community pressures boys.

What they struggle to accept is that a boy can ignore his father and follow the crowd.

Because we want to believe we are stronger than that.

We want to believe our families can protect us from everything.

We want to believe a father's warning is enough.

But in my case, it was not enough, because I was not wise enough to listen.

The dedication in the earlier version says it plainly. My father, Maluth Abiel Kueth, advised me against receiving the marks, and I ignored him because of peer pressure.

That sentence is simple, but it contains a whole tragedy.

Not only the tragedy of a boy's injury.

The tragedy of a boy's mind being captured by public opinion.

When I admitted that openly, I knew some people would laugh at me.

I also knew some people would respect the honesty.

But I did not have the luxury of hiding behind pride anymore, because if I hide my weakness, I will produce weak sons who pretend to be strong.

So I chose honesty.

Section: The moment writing became responsibility

At first, writing was survival.

It was my way of putting chaotic memory into order.

It was my way of speaking to myself without needing an audience.

Later, writing became responsibility.

Because autobiography is not only about self-expression. It can also be a bridge between generations, a way of preserving legacy, and a way of linking the past with the future.

That sentence captures what I began to feel in my bones.

A story that stays in one man's head dies with him.

A story that is written becomes a tool.

A tool can protect.

A tool can warn.

A tool can teach.

A tool can also heal, because it tells the next person, you are not alone, and you are not crazy for feeling what you feel.

This is why I eventually allowed the story to leave my hands.

Section: "This is not a fully researched account" and why that honesty matters

Some people want a personal story to sound like a university thesis.

They want footnotes for every sentence.

They want every detail confirmed by an archive.

But there is a danger in pretending you are doing something you are not doing.

The earlier version states that interviews were conducted, but it is not presented as a thoroughly researched account, and it stands as a personal narrative.

I respect that honesty because it protects the reader from confusion.

This book is not claiming to be the final authority on every history of scarification.

It is claiming to be a truthful account of what I lived, what I saw, what others told me, and what I learned from it.

That kind of truth is not small.

In many places, especially in our region, lived testimony often holds more practical value than polished theory, because testimony forces people to face real outcomes: blood loss, infection risk, pressure, regret, discrimination, pride, and the complex human feelings that live inside the same practice.

So I did not pretend to be an encyclopaedia.

I wrote as a man who survived and learned.

Section: The public world does not read scars the way home does

When the story left my hands, it entered a wider world.

And that wider world reads scars differently.

At home, the marks can be read as identity, lineage, and belonging.

The earlier work notes that facial markings can represent lineage, tribe, social standing, and solidarity, and can even function as protective markers in times of conflict.

212

But outside, those same marks can be read wrongly.

Outside, a scarred forehead can be treated as a symbol of violence.

Outside, scars can trigger stereotypes.

Outside, people can create false stories about your intelligence, your education, your values, and your humanity.

This is where I began to understand that telling my story publicly was also a way of correcting misreadings, not by begging for approval, but by speaking clearly.

It was also why I became careful with language, because mistranslation can create harmful stereotypes, and accurate translation plus open dialogue can prevent people from building hatred out of ignorance.

When your face is easy to misread, your words must be steady.

Section: The first reactions were not always fair

I learned something quickly.

The moment you speak publicly, people stop listening only to what you said and start listening to what they want to hear.

Some people heard my story and thought I was insulting our people.

Some heard it and thought I was insulting those who still carry scars with pride.

Some heard it and thought I was calling the practice evil, even when I was simply describing harm and pressure.

Some heard it and thought I was defending scarification, even when I was warning about coercion and health risks.

This confusion is partly why the work says it aims to be stimulating and educational rather than an encyclopedic account.

Education is slower than shouting.

Education can sound weak to those who love slogans.

But education is the only path that gives people room to think without humiliation.

So when reactions were unfair, I did not stop.

I adjusted my tone.

I clarified.

I learned to speak in a way that protects the child at the center of the matter.

Section: The question I began asking every listener

When people reacted strongly, I started using one question that cuts through politics.

Would you want your own child pressured into this?

Not your neighbor's child.

Not a boy you do not know.

Your own child.

Because it is easy to defend a practice when the pain is happening to someone else.

It becomes harder when the pain is personal.

That is why, in the "Dearest daughter" message, I made a direct promise that her brothers would not suffer the same fate.

That promise is not only emotional.

It is the measuring stick of my sincerity.

If I cannot protect my own children, then my public words are empty.

Section: How publication became part of the story

When a book is published, people think the story is finished.

In reality, publication is another chapter.

Because once a story has been printed, it can travel further than the author can travel.

It can enter rooms where the author is not present to explain.

It can enter hands that do not like the author.

It can enter communities that will try to use the story for their own agendas.

That is why I see publication as part of the autobiography itself, not only as a technical step.

The earlier file records the publication details and copyright in 2013, including Discipleship Press, a P.O. Box in Nairobi, and contact lines.

Those lines look administrative, but they represent a real season of my life.

They represent the moment I stopped hiding the story inside family talk and allowed it to exist as a public object.

They also represent the fact that my life and my writing have crossed places, and that my identity has had to live in more than one setting.

So publication was not the end.

It was the moment the story began living beyond my control.

Section: What I feared when I released the story

I feared two things.

The first fear was that outsiders would use my story to mock South Sudanese communities, to call us backward, to treat us as less human.

This is why I keep returning to the need for accurate language and open dialogue, because mistranslation and misunderstanding can turn into stereotypes, and stereotypes can turn into discrimination and even violence.

The second fear was that insiders would treat my story as betrayal.

Because there are people who believe that speaking about internal harm is the same as hating your people.

But if we refuse to speak about harm, we turn love into silence, and silence becomes another weapon against children.

So I accepted the risk.

I chose to trust that truth spoken with respect can still serve the community.

Section: The part many people avoid, the health risk

One reason I kept insisting on honesty is that the body does not forgive lies.

The earlier work speaks directly about infections and complications, and about the risk of transmission of HIV or Hepatitis B.

It also speaks about modern sterilization methods and disposable instruments as ways to reduce risk, while admitting that access and affordability can be difficult.

When I read those lines, I do not read them like a distant commentator.

I read them as someone who bled severely and reached a point where I seemed lifeless.

So when the story left my hands, I was not only telling the cultural side.

I was also refusing to hide the physical dangers.

Not to scare people.

To protect children, and to push adults into responsibility.

If a community chooses to keep the practice, then safety must become serious.

And if safety cannot be assured, then coercion must stop at once.

That is a moral line for me.

Section: The interviews and why I wanted other voices inside the book

Another thing that helped me release the story is that I did not want the book to sound like a man speaking alone in anger.

I wanted it to include voices and places, to show that this is a shared discussion, not a personal fight.

The earlier work includes interviews across multiple areas, including Upper Nile settings, Nasir, Malakal, and Goli at Emmanuel Christian Training Centre.

Those conversations helped me in two ways.

One, they reminded me that not everyone experiences scarification the same way.

Two, they helped me speak with more restraint, because when you have heard other people's mixed feelings, you stop using simple slogans.

And it also confirmed what the book states clearly: there is an ongoing debate, and the community itself carries different views, not one single voice.

So the story leaving my hands did not mean I was throwing stones at my people.

It meant I was entering a conversation that already existed.

Section: The kind of peace I was chasing while writing

Part V is not a call for civil war inside culture.

It is a call for a certain kind of peace.

Not silence.

Not fear.

Not fake unity.

A peace where a boy can belong without being cut.

217

A peace where a father can protect his child without being mocked.

A peace where elders can keep dignity while letting go of cruelty.

A peace where discussion can happen without humiliation.

That is why, in the message to my daughter, I could speak with tenderness and firmness at once, promising protection for her brothers and explaining that as a girl she would not be expected to bear the worst facial markings.

That is the peace that guided my writing.

And it is the peace that helped me release the story into public life.

Section: What I learned after the story became public

I learned that you cannot control readers.

You can only control your honesty.

I learned that some people will love your story for the wrong reasons, using it to mock others.

I learned that some people will hate your story for the wrong reasons, accusing you of betrayal.

I learned that the safest place is not popularity.

The safest place is a clean conscience.

And I learned that the story leaving my hands did not remove my responsibility.

It increased it.

Because once you publish, you must live in a way that matches what you wrote.

If you write about protecting children, you must protect them.

If you write about resisting pressure, you must resist it.

If you write about truth, you must not become a liar in your private life.

That is why I keep returning to the promise in the letter to my daughter.

It is not only a line of writing.

It is a covenant I must live.

Section: Where Chapter 20 leaves us

This chapter explains the shift.

The story left my hands.

It entered public space.

It began to meet misreadings, unfair reactions, and also sincere listeners.

It became part of my responsibility as a father and as a man who must build a safer future.

Part V still has more ground to cover.

In Chapter 21, we will move further into how I wanted this story to function inside our community and beyond it, not as a weapon, but as a bridge between generations and a protection for the young.

CHAPTER 21: WHAT I HOPE THIS BOOK DOES TO US

The last chapter is not the end of the work.

If you are reading this chapter, then you have carried my story with me from the blood of childhood into the conscience of adulthood.

This chapter is the last chapter of the book, but it is not the end of the work.

A book can close, but a society continues.

A scar can stop bleeding, but the questions around it continue.

A father can promise protection, but pressure can return in new clothes.

So I am not writing this as a perfect conclusion where everything becomes simple and clean. I am writing it as the clearest statement of what I wanted this book to do in the minds of those who read it, especially among my own people in South Sudan and among those outside who have only seen our faces and never sat with our hearts.

In the manuscript, I already said clearly that this is not meant to be a thoroughly researched account, even though I conducted interviews, and that it stands as a personal narrative. That honesty matters to me, because it tells you what kind of truth you are holding.

You are holding the truth of lived experience.

You are holding the truth of a boy pressured into pain.

You are holding the truth of a man who later became a father and refused to pass that pain down.

You are holding the truth of a people still debating what they love and what they fear.

That is enough to make a difference, if we do not treat it like entertainment.

Section: I want this book to remove the lies we use to recruit children

One of the most dangerous things in any society is a beautiful lie used to recruit children into harm.

When boys are young, they are hungry for belonging. They are hungry for approval. They are hungry for the feeling that they are not less than anyone else.

A community can use that hunger to build responsibility, or it can use that hunger to build obedience without thought.

I want this book to expose the lies we tell boys when we push them toward scarification.

The first lie is that pain automatically produces a man.

Pain can produce endurance, yes, but pain can also produce bitterness, trauma, and a false pride that hides insecurity. The manuscript itself associates scarification with training composure, endurance, and self-control, but the deeper question is what we do with those qualities. Endurance alone is not virtue. Endurance must be guided toward something good.

The second lie is that a boy who refuses is less human.

That lie is one of the most cruel lies we have allowed to live among us, because it turns the community into a prison. The text warns about social pressure and argues that the decision should be personal rather than driven by external pressure. I want that line to become a moral rule inside our social behavior, not a sentence we praise while continuing to shame boys.

The third lie is that the danger is exaggerated.

Some people speak as if there is no serious harm, as if it is only a temporary pain and then life continues. But my own experience included severe bleeding and a moment when I appeared lifeless and could not respond to people's questions. That is not a small detail. It is the kind of detail that should stop adults from speaking casually about the practice in front of children.

The fourth lie is that this is how it has always been, and therefore it must always be.

But the manuscript itself records that practices can shift across time, even within the same broader culture, noting that some age groups did not practice scarification and later age groups adopted it. That means change is not foreign to us. Adjustment is already part of our history. We only need the courage to guide adjustment toward protecting life and dignity.

If this book does nothing else, I want it to remove these lies from our public talk, because lies are the first blades that cut children long before any metal touches skin.

Section: I want this book to restore respect to the father's voice

There is a reason I keep returning to my father.

My father, Maluth Abiel Kueth, advised me against receiving the marks, and I ignored him because of peer pressure. That sentence is painful to write, because it contains both love and failure.

My father was trying to protect me.

The crowd was trying to shape me.

I chose the crowd.

That is not only my personal failure. It is also a warning about what happens when a society weakens the authority of parents and strengthens the authority of peers.

A boy does not need peers more than he needs protection.

Peers can be good, yes, but peers can also be cruel. Peers can become a mob. Peers can demand sacrifices in the name of belonging.

So I want this book to return honor to the father who says no when no is needed, even if the crowd calls him weak.

I want it to give courage to the mother who cries quietly but fears to speak because she does not want to be labeled as the one who is spoiling her son.

I want this book to remind parents that a child's future is not a community trophy.

Your child is your responsibility before he is the community's symbol.

If the community truly loves children, it will stop demanding that parents surrender them to shame and harm.

Section: I want this book to protect scarred men from being turned into jokes or monsters

There are two cruel ways people treat scarred men.

One cruelty is internal. Some of our own people use scars as a reason to mock those who are not scarred. They treat scars as a passport to respect and use them to dominate.

The other cruelty is external. Some outsiders see scars and treat the person as a savage, as if a marked face is proof of a low mind or a violent nature.

Both cruelties are wrong, and both reduce a human being to a symbol.

The manuscript recognizes that facial markings can function as symbols of solidarity and belonging and can convey information within communities, but it also recognizes negative consequences such as discrimination and psychological weight, especially when people are judged unfairly in modern settings.

So I want this book to do something humane.

I want it to protect the dignity of scarred men by telling the truth about how many of us received these marks when we were too young to fully consent, and how many of us were pressured by ridicule and exclusion.

If you are a scarred man reading this, I do not want you to hate your face.

Your face is your history.

Your face is also your testimony.

But I also do not want you to use your face as a weapon against boys who do not want scars.

Do not repeat the cruelty that hurt you.

If you are an unscarred man reading this, I do not want you to mock scarred men.

Mockery is cheap and it does not heal anything. It only creates another cycle of pride and defense.

If you are an outsider reading this, I do not want you to treat scarification as your excuse to insult an entire people.

If you truly care about human dignity, then speak with humility, not with superiority.

A scar is not proof of stupidity.

A scar is proof that human beings are shaped by cultures, pressures, histories, and sometimes by pain they did not fully choose.

Section: I want this book to make our debate more mature

In South Sudan, we often argue with heat. We often think the louder voice is the stronger voice.

But heat is not maturity.

Maturity is the ability to look at a practice and ask honest questions without turning those questions into tribal insults or family insults.

The manuscript describes the ongoing debate among South Sudanese themselves, including defense of scarification as heritage and condemnation tied to health and human rights concerns. I want this book to raise the level of that debate.

I want us to stop speaking like we are enemies.

I want us to stop speaking like every question is betrayal.

I want us to stop speaking like every defense is backwardness.

Instead, I want us to speak like people who understand that identity and protection can be carried together, if we have discipline.

This is why the manuscript speaks about balancing pride in heritage with dignity and respect, and it raises the tension of whether to abandon, hide, or stand firm while seeking recognition.

That is not an easy tension.

But maturity means we do not run away from hard tensions.

We face them.

We hold them.

We guide them.

We build with them.

Section: I want this book to make health a serious part of cultural responsibility

I will be direct here.

If any practice involves cutting skin, health must be part of the conversation.

This is not a foreign idea.

It is a human idea.

Even before modern hospitals, our elders knew what infection can do. They used herbs. They used methods of care. They understood that wounds can kill.

So why would we treat health talk as an insult now?

The manuscript mentions infections and complications and also raises risks of HIV or Hepatitis B transmission. It also discusses modern sterilization and disposable instruments as ways to reduce risk, while acknowledging challenges of access and affordability.

I want those lines to become part of public responsibility.

Not whispered.

Not ignored.

Not treated like an enemy attack.

If a community continues scarification, then it must treat safety as a minimum requirement, not as an optional improvement.

If safety cannot be assured, then coercion becomes even more indefensible.

I know what I am saying because I remember severe bleeding and collapse. No father should be casual about this.

No elder should be casual about this.

No community should be casual about this.

A child is not an experiment.

Section: I want this book to teach that choice must be real, not theatrical

Many communities say the right words but practice the wrong behavior.

They say, it is a choice.

Then they mock the boy who refuses.

They say, it is voluntary.

Then they exclude the unscarred boy from social acceptance.

They say, it is about identity.

Then they treat identity like a tool for domination.

This book has one moral line that I want to become normal in our thinking: the decision should be personal and not driven by external pressure.

If a decision is personal, then refusal must be respected.

If refusal is not respected, then the decision is not personal.

It is forced.

And a forced practice is not heritage.

It is control.

This is where I believe many societies fail.

We want the appearance of tradition, but we do not want the discipline of protecting conscience.

We want the symbol of unity, but we do not want the labor of building unity through respect.

So I want this book to push us toward a simple test.

When a boy refuses, do you still treat him as fully human?

If the answer is no, then the community is not practicing honor. It is practicing humiliation.

And humiliation will eventually return to burn the community itself, because humiliation produces resentment, and resentment does not build peace.

Section: I want this book to help outsiders understand without becoming judges

I have met outsiders who reacted to scars with curiosity and respect. I have also met outsiders who reacted with mockery.

Both reactions can be careless if they are not rooted in understanding.

I do not want outsiders to romanticize our scars like art on a wall while ignoring the pressure and health risks.

I also do not want outsiders to condemn us like they have never practiced harmful things in their own societies.

Every society has its own scars.

Some scars are on faces.

Some scars are on minds.

Some scars are on women's bodies through forced practices that people defended for centuries.

Some scars are on children through wars started by men in suits.

Some scars are invisible, but they destroy lives.

So if you are an outsider reading this, I want you to read with humility.

Ask questions.

Listen.

Do not assume you know everything because you have a degree or a passport.

At the same time, do not stay silent about harm.

Silence does not protect children.

So I want you to find the human balance: respect the dignity of the people, while standing for the dignity of the child.

Section: I want this book to correct mistranslation and the stereotypes born from it

One of the painful lessons of my life is that people can hate you because they misunderstood a word.

They can hate you because they mistranslated your term for manhood.

They can hate you because someone told them a story about your culture that is half true and half poison.

The manuscript warns about mistranslations and misunderstandings and calls for accurate translation and open dialogue, giving an example where a term was wrongly translated in a way that fueled stereotypes.

I want this book to become part of that open dialogue, because a scarred face often becomes a target for stereotype, and stereotype is a seed of discrimination.

If we correct language, we reduce unnecessary hatred.

If we correct misunderstandings, we reduce unnecessary fear.

If we explain ourselves accurately, we help people see the human story behind the marks.

This is not only for outsiders.

It is also for us inside South Sudan.

We have many languages. We have many tribes. We have many ways of naming things. When we mistranslate each other, we can build suspicion where there should be unity.

So I want this book to teach one simple habit: before you judge, ask what a word truly means in its home language.

Section: I want this book to honor the voices of others, not only my own voice

I did not want this book to sound like one man shouting alone.

That is why I conducted interviews and conversations across different places and with different people, even while admitting the work is personal narrative. The interview list in the manuscript includes multiple settings in Upper Nile, Nasir, Malakal, and Goli at Emmanuel Christian Training Centre.

Those locations matter because they represent something larger than geography.

They represent the truth that scarification is not one uniform practice and not one uniform feeling. People carry it differently. People defend it differently. People regret it differently.

Some men carry pride.

Some carry regret.

Some carry mixed feelings that they do not know how to express.

The manuscript even includes the voice of a man who wished he could remove his scars, even though they were not very visible.

I want that kind of quiet voice to be heard.

Because societies often listen only to loud voices, and loud voices are not always the most truthful voices.

So if this book makes space for quieter truths, then it is doing something good.

Section: I want this book to become a bridge between generations

I wrote earlier that autobiography can preserve legacy and link generations. That is not a fancy phrase for me. It is a practical task.

I do not want my children to inherit my pain as a mystery they cannot name.

I want them to know what happened, how it happened, why it happened, and what I chose to do with the lesson.

That is why I wrote to my daughter when she was five months old. That letter is not only a tender section. It is the evidence of a father's moral shift, and it is a record of a promise that must outlive emotion.

I told her that her brothers would not suffer the same fate as I did, marked with scars. That promise is the bridge.

It is the bridge between a wounded boy and a protecting father.

It is the bridge between old pressure and new discipline.

It is the bridge between inherited practice and chosen responsibility.

I want this book to function like that bridge for other families too.

I want it to help a father speak to his sons without shame.

I want it to help a mother speak to her husband without fear.

I want it to help an elder consider a new approach without feeling humiliated.

I want it to help a young man understand that real manhood is not proven by injury.

This is how a story becomes bigger than one man.

It becomes part of a shared education.

Section: I want this book to encourage alternative ways of teaching manhood

Some people fear that if scarification is questioned, then manhood will disappear.

That fear is understandable, because rites of passage are not only about the body. They are about belonging. They are about responsibility. They are about discipline.

But the question is not whether boys need guidance.

The question is what kind of guidance produces good men.

If scarification is defended because it trains endurance and self-control, then we must ask a deeper question.

Can endurance be trained without injury?

Can self-control be trained without blood?

Can discipline be trained without forcing children into irreversible choices?

I believe the answer is yes.

We can build rites of passage that teach boys to serve.

We can build rites of passage that teach boys to protect women and children.

We can build rites of passage that teach boys to work, to study, to keep promises, to resist revenge, to resist tribal arrogance, to respect elders without surrendering conscience.

Those are the qualities that build a nation.

A scar on a face does not automatically build those qualities.

A rite of passage that truly trains character can build them, whether or not it uses a blade.

So I want this book to free our imagination.

Not to destroy identity.

To strengthen it by removing what harms and keeping what builds.

Section: I want this book to be honest about how complicated identity can feel

There is a temptation in cultural debates to present identity like a clean thing.

This is who we are.

This is what we do.

This is what proves it.

But real identity is not clean. It is lived. It is emotional. It is sometimes contradictory.

A man can be proud of his people and still regret a practice.

A man can be scarred and still wish he could remove the marks.

A man can defend heritage and still fear for his children's safety.

A man can criticize coercion and still love his elders.

A man can travel and learn and still want to come home.

I want this book to allow those complicated feelings to exist without shame, because shame is one of the greatest enemies of honest growth.

When shame controls a society, people become actors.

They perform loyalty.

They perform toughness.

They perform agreement.

But inside, they suffer quietly.

I want less performance and more truth.

Truth is not always comfortable, but it is the beginning of healing.

Section: I want this book to make you look at a scarred face differently

If you see a scarred face after reading this, I want you to pause before you assume.

Do not assume the man is uneducated.

Do not assume the man is violent.

Do not assume the man is proud of the scars.

Do not assume the man regrets them.

Do not assume you know his story.

Instead, understand this.

A scarred face may be carrying a childhood decision shaped by pressure.

A scarred face may be carrying a story of severe bleeding and near collapse.

A scarred face may be carrying loyalty to heritage and also a fear for his children.

A scarred face may be carrying regret that he never says aloud because men are trained to hide.

A scarred face may be carrying pride that is not arrogance but survival.

So look at the scarred face with humanity.

If you are from the same culture, do not use the scar to dominate others.

If you are from outside, do not use the scar to dehumanize.

If you are a parent, do not use the scar to recruit your child into the same pressure.

If you are a young person, do not let the scar become the proof you think you must buy.

Section: I want this book to put responsibility where it belongs

There are people who like to blame everything on culture, as if culture is a monster that acts by itself.

But culture is carried by human beings.

Culture is maintained by choices.

Culture is enforced by behavior.

So responsibility belongs to us.

It belongs to elders who shame children.

It belongs to young men who mock their peers.

It belongs to fathers who surrender to pressure.

It belongs to mothers who stay silent when they know harm is happening.

It belongs to leaders who refuse to guide society toward safer ways.

It belongs to all of us.

That is why I do not like easy condemnation.

Easy condemnation is laziness.

It allows us to feel morally superior without changing anything.

I want this book to produce real responsibility, the kind that changes behavior.

Responsibility means we stop the mockery.

Responsibility means we protect freedom of refusal.

Responsibility means we treat safety seriously.

Responsibility means we stop turning children into symbols.

Responsibility means we teach manhood by character, not by coercion.

Section: I want this book to be read as love, not as insult

Some people will read this book and feel attacked.

If you are one of them, let me speak directly.

My intent is not to insult you.

My intent is to protect children and keep dignity intact.

I understand why people defend scarification as heritage. When a people have been attacked, mocked, displaced, and misunderstood, identity markers can feel like the last wall between them and erasure. The manuscript acknowledges that facial markings can function as symbols of solidarity and belonging. I do not ignore that.

But I also refuse to ignore the harm, the pressure, and the health risk.

So this book is an attempt to hold both truths.

To honor the dignity of the people.

To protect the dignity of the child.

If you read it as insult, you may miss the purpose.

If you read it as love with discipline, you may find a way forward that does not require humiliation or blood.

Section: Why I believe the future can be better than the past

Some people believe nothing changes.

They believe pressure is permanent.

They believe the crowd will always win.

They believe children will always be used.

But I do not believe that.

I do not believe that because I have already seen change inside my own life.

I did not listen to my father once.

Later, I became a father and wrote a promise to my daughter that her brothers would not suffer the same fate.

That is change.

Not perfect change.

But real change.

And if one man can change, a community can change too.

The manuscript also hints, through its own historical notes, that practices have shifted across time and age sets.

So we are not trapped.

We can keep dignity.

We can keep identity.

We can keep unity.

We can also keep children safe.

We only need courage and discipline.

Section: A final word to the young man who is deciding

If you are a young man standing at that crossroad, feeling the pressure, hearing the jokes, fearing exclusion, hear me clearly.

Belonging bought by injury is expensive.

What looks like a quick entry ticket can become a lifelong weight.

If you choose scarification as an adult with full understanding and real freedom, that is your decision.

But if you are being pushed, mocked, and cornered, then that is not freedom.

Do not confuse coercion with culture.

A culture worth carrying should not need to bully you.

If a community wants you to belong, it should make belonging possible without harm.

That is my appeal to you.

Protect your future.

And do not let fear of people become the ruler of your body.

Section: A final word to the parents

If you are a parent, I want you to remember something.

The crowd will not raise your child.

You will.

The crowd will not carry the regret if something goes wrong.

You will.

The crowd will not pay the cost if infection happens.

You will.

The crowd will not repair your son's future if he later regrets what happened.

You will.

So stand firm.

If you want to protect your child, protect him.

Do not outsource your fatherhood to mockery.

Do not outsource your motherhood to fear.

You can respect elders and still protect your child.

If elders are wise, they will respect your protection.

If elders are not wise, then your protection becomes even more necessary.

Section: A final word to the elders

If you are an elder, I want to honor you and challenge you at the same time.

You have carried us through hard years.

You have carried our stories.

You have carried our identity.

But identity is not strengthened by forcing children into pain through humiliation.

Identity is strengthened by teaching character and unity.

Identity is strengthened when the weak are protected.

Identity is strengthened when boys can refuse without being treated as less.

If you want to preserve what is valuable in our heritage, preserve it with wisdom.

Do not preserve it with cruelty.

The world is changing, yes, but a wise elder does not fear change blindly.

A wise elder guides change so that dignity remains.

Section: The last sentence I want to leave inside your mind

I cannot remove my scars.

But I can refuse to pass their pain down.

That is why I wrote this book.

That is why I spoke to people in different places and listened.

That is why I told the truth about pressure.

That is why I told the truth about the blood and the collapse.

That is why I wrote to my daughter and promised protection.

If this book helps even one family protect a child from being forced, then it has done something worth doing.

If it helps even one elder choose wisdom over humiliation, then it has served dignity.

If it helps even one outsider see our faces with humanity instead of stereotype, then it has corrected a small part of the world.

And if it helps you, the reader, understand that a scar is not only a mark, but a story, then you have read it the way I hoped you would.

CLOSING
THE SCAR THAT BECAME A TEACHER

There are mornings when I stand in front of a mirror and I do not think of scarification at all. I wash my face. I clear my eyes. I adjust my collar. I step out and meet the day. The scars sit there quietly, like they always have. But there are other mornings when the mirror becomes a small courtroom, not the kind that condemns, but the kind that reminds. I stand there and the face looks back at me with two ages at once. The boy is still there, somewhere behind the skin, and the man is there too, standing in the same place, carrying a mind that has traveled further than the boy ever imagined.

When I was young, the scars felt like a ticket I had to buy. I thought manhood was a door that only opened with pain. I thought belonging was something you earn through blood. I did not know that some doors are traps, and some tickets are paid for by fear, not courage. I remember how quickly strength can leave a body, how the blood can pour until the world becomes far, how people can speak to you and you cannot answer, how you can appear lifeless in front of those who expected you to stand proud. That memory still visits, not as a punishment, but as a warning that pain is not poetry when it is real.

In the mirror now, the scars do not feel like a crown. They do not feel like shame either. They feel like a teacher that does not talk, a teacher that only points. It points to the day I ignored a father's counsel because of peer pressure. It points to the price of letting the crowd shape your body before your mind is mature. It points to the way identity can be used like a rope, pulling young people toward choices they do not fully understand. It points to the way people can read a face and decide they know the whole story, even when they know nothing.

But the mirror also points to the other side of the lesson. It points to the day I became a father and drew a line I wish I had drawn earlier. It points to the moment I wrote to my daughter, when she was only five months old, and promised that her brothers would not suffer the same fate of facial markings. In that promise, I did not erase my scars. I changed their meaning. I turned them from a wound into a boundary. I

240

turned them from a memory into a decision. I turned them from a mark of what happened to me into a warning about what must not happen again.

So when I look at my face now, older and clearer, I do not ask, what did the scars give me? I ask, what did they teach me? They taught me that courage without wisdom is danger. They taught me that belonging built on humiliation is not belonging. They taught me that a father's love can be ignored, but it should never be forgotten. They taught me that tradition is not holy when it harms the child and refuses correction. They taught me that a man can respect his people and still refuse to pass pain down. They taught me that the strongest form of manhood is not silence under a blade, but protection under pressure.

And in that mirror, the deepest peace is this. I cannot change the boy's choice. But I can change the father's choice. That is how the scar became a teacher.

HOW THIS BOOK FITS AUTOBIOGRAPHY SERIES

Book 7 sits inside my larger journey as the chapter of identity tested by pressure, choices made too young, consequences carried into adulthood, and growth that came later through honesty, responsibility, and fatherhood. It is the point where my face became a visible record of a decision, and where my life began learning how to turn regret into direction. In the wider Autobiography Series, this book connects the early formation of self to the later formation of conscience, showing that who we become is shaped not only by what happens to us, but by what we choose to do after it happens, and by how we protect the next generation from repeating the same costly lessons.

NEXT IN THE AUTOBIOGRAPHY SERIES

The road continues, and the next book follows the next turning point where identity meets a new test, and the cost of a choice shows itself in a different light.

ABOUT THE AUTHOR

John Monyjok Maluth is a South Sudanese writer whose Autobiography Series traces a life shaped by displacement, conflict, faith, learning, and hard-won self-understanding. He writes with honesty about the moments that formed him, not to polish the past, but to make meaning from it and to leave a clear record for the next generation. His work centers on identity, responsibility, and the simple truth that growth begins when a person tells the whole story.